D1037681

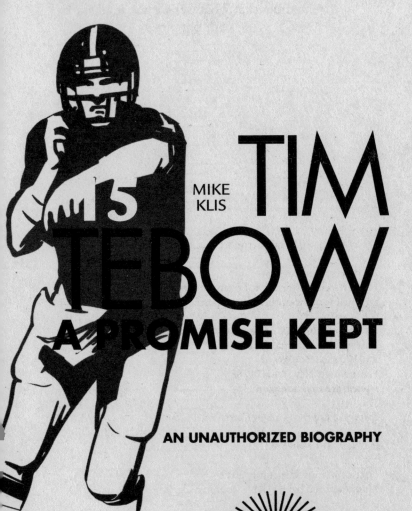

MIKE
KLIS

TIM TEBOW
A PROMISE KEPT

AN UNAUTHORIZED BIOGRAPHY

BARRON'S

Dedication

To Mom and Dad. For all you youngsters out there,
remember that whatever we are, it all starts
with parents.

All inquiries should be addressed to:
Barron's Educational Series, Inc.
250 Wireless Boulevard
Hauppauge, New York 11788
www.barronseduc.com

Library of Congress Catalog Card No.: 2012944103

ISBN: 978-1-4380-0212-5

Date of Manufacture: July 2012
Manufactured by: B11R11, Robbinsville, NJ

Printed in the United States of America

9 8 6 5 4 3 2 1

Contents

Chapter 1

Tebow, Now a New York Jet

O n March 26, 2012, Tim Tebow entered the New York Jets' indoor practice field facility in Florham Park, New Jersey, wearing a Jet-green tie, a well-tailored gray suit, a fashionable two-day stubble, and his ever-present grin.

"It's such an honor for me to be here," Tebow greeted the throng of New York press there to meet and question him. "I'm so excited about being a Jet."

To many, witnessing Tebow introduced as a new player with the New York Jets was unusual, if not startling. After his sensational career at the University of Florida, one of the best in college football history, Tebow was selected by the Denver Broncos in the first round of the 2010 NFL draft. Many football experts were surprised Tebow had been drafted that highly. They said Tebow would fail as a pro quarterback because of his seriously flawed passing motion.

Tebow's achievements in his first two seasons, particularly in 2011, proved his critics wrong. Tebow played well in his three-game audition to finish his rookie year with the Broncos. Still, the Broncos' new management team operations director John Elway and head coach John Fox were skeptical. A competition in training camp led to veteran Kyle Orton getting the starting quarterback job for the third consecutive season.

But by the end of the 2011 season, Tebow was not only

playing, but playing so well that he became the most talked about player in the NFL. Tebow pulled out miracle win after miracle win with clutch, fourth-quarter performances, often in the final minutes of the game. He led a Broncos team that was so bad, it had not reached the playoffs in six years. He led a Broncos team that was so bad, the year before, in 2010, it tied for the league's second-worst record. He led a Broncos team that was so bad in 2011, it started the season with a 1–4 record with Orton as the starter.

Yet, from the time Tebow became the Broncos' starting quarterback in Game 6 of the 2011 season, the team then won seven of its next eight games. That 7–1 run included a six-game winning streak that was enough to lift the Broncos to the AFC West Division title and a playoff berth in the postseason.

In the playoffs, Tebow had arguably his best game as a pro, throwing for 316 yards to defeat the heavily favored Pittsburgh Steelers, 29–23 in overtime, at the Broncos' home of Sports Authority Field at Mile High. The winning score came on the first and the last play of overtime when Tebow threw a perfectly accurate pass to Demaryius Thomas down the middle of the field.

A charter franchise of the American Football League in 1960, the Denver Broncos played their home games at Mile High Stadium for 41 years. Its name came from the fact that Denver is located a mile above sea level. John Elway played his entire 16-year NFL career (1983–98) with Mile High as his home. A new replacement stadium hosted its first regular-season game under the name Invesco Field at Mile High on Sept. 10, 2001 against the New York Giants. The Broncos defeated the Giants, 31–20, on the nationally televised Monday Night Football program. The next morning, terrorists attacked the United States, a day that will be forever known as 9-11. The stadium's name was changed to Sports Authority Field at Mile High in 2011.

Thomas was also drafted by the Broncos in the first round of the 2010 draft. Thomas, a receiver from Georgia Tech, was selected with the No. 22 overall pick. Tebow went at No. 25.

And now No. 25 and No. 22 were hooking up for one of the most electric plays the Broncos had executed since they moved into their new stadium in 2001.

After Thomas caught the long pass, Tebow watched as the receiver stiff-armed his way from one tackler, cornerback Ike Taylor and outran another, safety Ryan Mundy. Thomas didn't stop until he reached the end zone for an 80-yard touchdown.

After the play, Tebow bolted down the middle of the field, delirious with joy. "Thank you, Lord! Thank you, Lord!" Tebow repeated as he ran. He finally reached the south end zone of the stadium, the same end zone that Thomas had scored the game-winning touchdown moments before. Tebow ran out of the back of the end zone and jumped to the top of the ledge bordering the stands. Fans in the front row had the honor of slapping their hero on the back, on his helmet, on whatever they could hit. It was the first time Tebow had ever jumped into the stands, now a common practice among NFL players.

"The fans were so excited," Tebow said. "It felt good, but they were so excited, I didn't know if they were going to let me go."

The "Mile High Leap," followed by his customary

> The tradition of players jumping into the stands following a touchdown began on Dec. 26, 1993 when Green Bay Packers' great Reggie White picked up a fumble by the Los Angeles Raiders, then lateraled to safety Leroy Butler. After sprinting in the final 25 yards for a touchdown, Butler spontaneously ran through the end zone and leaped into the stands at Lambeau Field, the Packers home stadium. The so-called "Lambeau Leap" was born. Today, players on all teams often celebrate by leaping into the stands to share their joy with their fans.

3

kneel in prayer to give thanks, would be Tebow's final act before his home fans as a Denver Bronco. For despite cramming a lifetime of heroics into a single season, despite singlehandedly generating excitement in what had been a discouraged Denver community, and despite making the Broncos relevant on a national stage, Tebow was traded to the Jets just two months after his magical season.

The Broncos didn't give up on Tebow, exactly. The team first signed superstar quarterback Peyton Manning from free agency. Manning is considered not only one of the best quarterbacks currently playing in the NFL, he is often mentioned as perhaps the best quarterback of all time.

Manning became available in free agency because of a series of unusual circumstances. It was one domino that fell into another that eventually landed Manning in Denver.

First, Manning suffered a neck injury in 2010 that required four surgeries. The neck issue was so serious, he was forced to miss the entire 2011 season. In his absence, the Colts finished with the worst record in the NFL at 2–14.

The Colts' terrible year came at a time when sensational college quarterback Andrew Luck of Stanford became eligible for the draft. Many football experts considered Luck the best quarterback prospect since a Tennessee quarterback named Peyton Manning entered the draft in 1998. Others said Luck was the best NFL quarterback prospect since John Elway left Stanford in 1983.

Ironically, Luck, Manning, and Elway all came together in 2012 to essentially push Tebow out of Denver and to New York City, the most populated city in the United States.

New York is the most populous U.S. city with 19 million people in its metropolitan area, according to the 2010 U.S. Census. Los Angeles is a distant second with 12.9 million. Rounding out the top five cities in terms of metro-area population are Chicago, Dallas, and Houston. Denver has the 21st most populated metro area with 2.6 million.

The Indianapolis Colts decided they would select Luck with the No. 1 overall pick in the draft, leading to Manning's release from the Colts. Once Manning became a free agent, at least 10 teams bid for his services. He eventually narrowed his choices to four: Tennessee Titans, San Francisco 49ers, Arizona Cardinals, and the Broncos. On March 19, 2012, Manning announced his intention to play for the Broncos. On the next day, March 20, the Broncos signed Manning to play for $18 million for the 2012 season.

On March 21, the day after they signed Manning, the Broncos traded their incumbent quarterback, Tim Tebow, to the New York Jets in exchange for one pick in the fourth round and another in the sixth round of the 2012 draft.

Publicly, Elway was extremely complimentary of Tebow after the trade was made.

> Manning is the only NFL player to win four Most Valuable Player awards. After 13 seasons in the league, Manning ranked No. 3 on the NFL all-time list in touchdown passes (399), passing yards (54,828), and pass completions. Brett Favre ranks first and Dan Marino second in each of those three passing categories.

"Our goal was to do the best thing for Tim and the Broncos, and I believe the opportunity that presented itself with the New York Jets accomplishes that objective," Elway said in a statement. "Tim made a lot of strides last year and has a very promising career ahead of him. If anyone is willing to put the work in to be great, it's Tim Tebow."

Privately, the Broncos believed Tebow's enormous popularity would be a distraction as the team moved forward in the Peyton Manning era. Tebow had so many devoted fans. If Manning struggled and the Broncos went through a stretch where they lost two in a row, the army of Tebow fans would be chanting: "Put in Tebow!"

That is what had happened during Tebow's first two years with the Broncos. Whatever the reasons, whatever the feelings, a decision was made. Peyton Manning was now the Broncos' quarterback. Tebow was now a New York Jet. For his part, Tebow was extremely gracious when he was introduced five days later, March 26, with a press conference at the Jets' practice facility.

"They got one of the best quarterbacks to ever play this game in Peyton Manning," Tebow said. "He's always been extremely classy and supportive of me. I wish him nothing but the best. There's no ill will towards the Broncos, Peyton Manning, or anybody."

That Tebow's press conference was held at the Jets' indoor field house was significant. The Jets had never held a press conference there. They had always used a large conference room inside their headquarters, which is located on the same campus in Florham Park.

But the Jets' public relations staff, headed by Bruce Speight, needed more room to accommodate the media crowd of more than 200. Included in that gathering were 36 camera people who occupied the first three rows, according to a SI.com story.

When Tebow became available for trade, it was not surprising that the Jets and Jacksonville Jaguars were the two teams most interested in acquiring his services. Jacksonville is Tebow's hometown. The team often struggled to sell out its home games so Tebow would have been a welcome draw to the Jaguars fans.

The Jets' interest in Tebow, though, was more about his on-field performance. While with the Broncos, Tebow played two games against the Jets, one in each season. He played well both times. The first game, on October 10, 2010, was Tebow's breakout game as an NFL player. The Jets rallied in the final seconds to beat the Broncos, 24–20, in Denver, but Tebow was effective in his first real game action. Used as an option quarterback, Tebow rushed for

23 yards rushing on six carries, including a 5-yard touchdown early in the second quarter.

Jets coach Rex Ryan noticed the unique way the Broncos coach used Tebow in the games. That same season, Ryan used Jets wide receiver Brad Smith in his "wildcat" formations to great success. The Jets finished the 2010 season ranked No. 4 in league rushing with 148.4 yards per game.

But after the 2010 season, Smith became a free agent and signed with the rival Buffalo Bills. The Jets' running game plummeted to No. 22 out of 32 teams in 2011. The team that led the NFL in rushing that year? That would be the Tebow-led Broncos. After a slow start in the running game with Kyle Orton at quarterback, the Broncos wound up running away, shall we say, with the rushing title with a whopping 164.5 yards per game.

The Jets acquired Tebow with the intent of having him back up starting quarterback Mark Sanchez. But he was also expected to run from the quarterback position in the so-called "wildcat" formation.

"We missed Brad Smith (a wide receiver who had run the wildcat formation before leaving the team the year before)," Jets general manager Mike Tannenbaum said at the NFL annual meetings in Palm Beach, Fla. "I didn't do a good job of replacing him. We want Tim to fill that role for us."

But it was the second time the Jets played against Tebow that convinced Ryan and Tannenbaum that he was a legitimate NFL quarterback. Nov. 17, 2011 was one of the most exciting games seen not only in Denver or New York, but also across the country. It was played on a Thursday night and was a prime time game shown on the NFL Network.

The Jets were ahead 13–10 with about 6 minutes left in the game. They had the Broncos pinned on their own 5-yard line. It seemed Ryan had finally solved the Tebow mystery. But something happens to Tebow late in games, especially when it appears his team is on the verge of certain defeat. Before the 2011 season would end, these situations would become commonly referred to as "Tebow Time."

Tebow rushed and passed the Broncos on a long drive. He finished with a 20-yard run for a touchdown with 58 seconds remaining. The Broncos won 17–13. A sellout crowd of 74,746 went berserk. The national cable audience was incredulous that Tebow had done it again.

Five months later, the quarterback who beat Ryan had now joined him. Tebow was a New York Jet.

In July, 2012, the Tebow to Thomas, 80-yard touchdown that beat the Steelers in the NFL playoff game was given the ESPY "Best Moment" award.

In his acceptance speech from the stage of the Los Angeles Nokia Theatre, Tebow graciously thanked his former teammates for the magical 2011 season they shared in Denver.

"Take care of them, Peyton," Tebow said.

Chapter 2

Born to Overcome

Timothy Richard Tebow was born on August 14, 1987. The date of the event was not as remarkable as the place where it occurred. His mother gave birth on the other side of the world from the United States, on the island nation of The Philippines. Tebow was born outside the capital city, Manila, in the Makiti City Medical Center.

Although his family moved from the Philippines to Jacksonville, Florida when Tim was just 3 years old, he still has a special place in his heart for the children of that tropical nation of 7,107 islands. From the time he was old enough to take missionary trips at age 15, Tebow has visited the Philippines several times. After his rookie season with the Denver Broncos, the Tim Tebow Foundation

As a result of the Spanish-American War, Spain ceded control of the Philippines to the victorious Americans. But the United States did not grant the Philippines their independence until 1946.

Manila, where Tim Tebow lived the first three years of his life, had a population in 2010 of more than 1.65 million. The city was most known to U.S. sports fans for the "Thrilla in Manila" heavyweight boxing match between Muhammad Ali and Joe Frazier in 1975—12 years before Tebow was born in the nearby suburb of Makati City. It was the third and final bout between the rivals. Both boxers were beaten up badly with Ali proclaimed the winner by TKO after the referee would not allow Frazier to come out for the 15th and final round.

teamed up with CURE (Crippled Children's United Rehabiliation Effort) International to develop a surgical facility and children's hospital in Davao City on the island of Mindanao, Philippines. The hospital will have 30 beds and treat such maladies as club foot and bow legs—which are correctable in the United States, but not in many areas of the Philippines.

"I'm excited to be a part of this hospital that will bring healing to thousands of children who would not otherwise have access to care," Tebow said when his foundation's involvement was announced.

Some of this aid came from the generosity that is part of Tebow's character. And some of it was personal. Tebow may not have become one of the country's most inspirational figures had his parents taken the advice of a doctor who practiced in a poor area of the Philippines.

Tebow's story really begins even before he was born. His father, Bob Tebow, has been a pastor and missionary for most of his life. In March 1971—16 years before Tim was born—Bob Tebow became the first from his family to graduate from the University of Florida. Make that a virtual tie. Because Bob's college sweetheart and future wife, Pam, graduated from Florida in June 1971.

Soon after their graduation, Bob and Pam were married and eventually had five children. Timothy—which means "honoring God" was the youngest.

In 1985, before Tim's birth, Bob was inspired to help the Filipino people learn about Christianity. More specifically, Bob Tebow wanted to minister in Mindanao, which is heavily populated with people of Muslim faith. However, Bob Tebow's life passion became the welfare of the orphaned children in Mindanao.

The Tebows and their four children—daughters Christy and Katie and sons Robby and Peter—moved to General Santos City on a primitive southern island of Mindanao.

When Pam became pregnant with Tim, she experienced extreme pain. A doctor in Mindanao said Pam Tebow would not survive if she carried on with the delivery of her baby.

The entire Tebow family turned to prayer several times a day. They also moved to Manila, where modern medicine and an American-trained doctor were available.

Tim was born in nearby Makati City. Tim and his mom needed a week's care in the hospital but both fully recovered. Later, when Tebow pulled off all those late-game rallies and fourth-quarter comebacks, no one should have been surprised. He'd been rallying since birth.

From his first day on earth, Tebow has been proving those who have doubted him wrong. The doctor in Mindanao was the first, if not the last.

Years later, as Tebow was in the final weeks of his sensational career for the University of Florida Gators, Jimmy Johnson was the first "expert" who said the college superstar would fail as an NFL quarterback.

Johnson was one of the most successful football coaches of all time, winning a national title for the University of Miami and then two Super Bowls for the Dallas Cowboys. He is now a NFL studio commentator for the Fox network.

Jimmy Johnson and Barry Switzer are the only coaches in history who have won both a national title in college and the Super Bowl. They were assistants to Oklahoma head coach Chuck Fairbanks from 1970–72. Johnson and Switzer each won their Super Bowls with the Dallas Cowboys. Both were hired by owner Jerry Jones. And both coaches wound up having their relationships with Jones sour.

Johnson won his NCAA Division I-A national championship with the University of Miami in 1987, and his Super Bowls with the Cowboys in 1992–93. Despite those back-to-back NFL championships, Johnson resigned prior to the 1994 season.

Jerry Jones replaced Johnson with Switzer, who had won NCAA titles with Oklahoma in 1974, 1975, and 1985. Switzer coached the Cowboys to a Super Bowl victory in the 1995 season. Switzer resigned two years later.

Johnson's credentials as both a college and NFL "expert" were superb. So when Johnson said he didn't like Tebow's chances of becoming a starting NFL quarterback, people listened.

"I don't think Tebow can play in a pro-style offense, not as a quarterback," Johnson said on the Dan Patrick radio show in late 2009. "I think a team that's going to look at Tim Tebow, they're going to make one of two decisions. If they're going to bring him into their style of play, with their coaching staff, they've got to project him to be maybe an H-back.

"I don't know if he's fast enough to be a receiver, maybe he could be a tight end. I don't know if he can block, I don't know if he can catch the ball. But he's got to play another position. He can't play quarterback." Perhaps if Johnson had known of Tebow's background, he never would have made such statements. Indeed, Johnson would soon soften his opinion and eventually become one of Tebow's biggest fans. Johnson's initial criticism didn't discourage Tebow because it was nothing new. When was the first time Tebow heard he couldn't play quarterback? It was the first time he played football in the local Pop Warner League.

After the Tebows first moved back to Jacksonville, Florida, Tim was not allowed to play football. He had played organized baseball at age 5 but it wasn't until three years later that his mom finally permitted him to play football. In his very first organized football game, Tebow played running back, which did not thrill him. But he played it as well as he could. Which was very well.

He would move to quarterback in his second Pop Warner game. But throughout his youth, his coaches thought that because of his large size, he would be better suited playing running back and linebacker.

As he was about to move up from Pop Warner to the Pee Wee League, again Tebow's coach said he was thinking of making Tim a fullback.

"Okay," Bob Tebow replied, according to Tim Tebow's autobiography, "Through My Eyes." I'm thinking about having Timmy play for another team."

The coach quickly saw the error of his ways and Tebow became his quarterback.

But the debate was never settled. Each time Tebow moved up a level of organized football, the question of whether he and the team were better off with him as quarterback would return.

As he matured, Tebow was homeschooled by his mother, but he needed to choose a high school to play team athletics. His first choice seemed easy enough—Jacksonville Trinity Christian Academy, the school where his two older brothers, Robby and Peter, attended.

In Tebow's freshman year, Trinity's coach insisted that Tim play linebacker as his brothers did before him. The coach believed Tim was too big to play quarterback.

Again, Tebow played linebacker without complaint but after his freshman year, he and his parents found another local high school where a coach would let him play quarterback. Nease Public High School had just hired an ex-college coach named Craig Howard. Nease was hardly a football powerhouse. In Tebow's first season there, his sophomore year, Nease played on the road in six different homecoming games. Schools generally schedule a weaker opponent for its homecoming game when the alumni return for various school activities and festivities. Nease filled the bill.

The Panthers greatly improved in their first year under Tebow and Coach Howard, but they lost five of their final six games and missed the playoffs.

Tebow was a star even in high school, but some were envious of his success. In a January 2012 story in Jacksonville's *The Florida Times-Union* newspaper that looked back on Tebow's high school career: *So polarizing was a 15- and 16-year-old Tebow that he elicited numerous letters to the editor in the* St. Augustine Record *newspaper. Rarely were they positive. One reader said that Tebow had "poor sportsmanship" and another said he "chokes" under pressure. Both letters were from adults.*

But in Tebow's senior year, he led the Nease Panthers to the state championship. Nease edged two-time defending champion Seffner Armwood 44–37 in the championship game. Tebow passed for 237 yards and four touchdowns and rushed for 153 yards and two more touchdowns. That added up to 390 yards and six touchdowns!

Tebow may not be perfect. Nobody is. But he definitely does not choke under pressure.

When the Tebows moved to Jacksonville in October 1990—just after Tim's third birthday—they settled in a home that his parents had owned since 1977. Within two years, Bob Tebow moved the family again, this time from the city to a farm. The primary reason for the change was that the Tebows needed more room for their growing family.

Another reason for the move was that Tebow's father did not believe in spoiling his children. He loved and supported them, but he believed in rearing them with strong character values. And behind great character is a strong work ethic. It would be almost impossible to operate a farm without a strong work ethic from all family members.

"It was such a blessing," Tebow said in the Broncos' cafeteria in January 2012, three days after his magical season had ended with a playoff loss at New England to the Patriots. "We got it at a government auction for way less than we could ever afford. It was a great place to have five kids grow up and work. I think that built as much character in us as anything else. Having to really grow up.

"My dad would leave the country and first it was Robby's responsibility to take care of the farm, but by the time I was 11 or 12, everybody would leave for five weeks in the summer to go to the Philippines. And it would just be me and my mom at the house because I was too young to go. So it was my responsibility from when I was 11 or 12 years old up until I was old enough to go (at 15) to the Philippines to take care of the cows, take care of the horses, take care of the chickens, take care of our garden, cut the grass."

As Tebow spoke, he became distracted and started laughing to himself. You could almost see his mind whir. The conversation caused him to reflect on the "good ol' days" on the farm.

He was asked: "What's so funny? What are you thinking about?" It was the garden.

"It was waaaay too big," Tebow said, chuckling. "My dad had that for misery. We would have corn, squash, zucchini, cucumbers, okra. And it was a ridiculous garden. It was like a half-acre garden. It was ridiculous to work in that."

The daily chores of the Tebow brothers included caring for the horses and the cows, tossing around bales of hay, and chopping wood. Even so, Tim found the time to play sports every day with his brothers. Baseball in the summer. Football in the fall. Basketball in winter.

One day in front of his Denver Broncos locker, Tebow said he would have never been the football player he became if not for playing with his older brothers nearly every day of his life.

Robby and Peter never let Tim win just because he was the youngest. They beat Tim in every game until he finally became old enough to beat them. The competition was fierce. But because Tim "played up" throughout his youth, he was always advanced for his age group.

"For Christmas (in 2011), my mom brought all these home videos I had never seen before," Tebow said. "They brought a whole stack of home videos. It has me at 2 years old in the Philippines running around, and my brothers were way bigger than I was, and Robby is just crushing me. I was running on the field holding a football and a baseball and Robby is decked out in this full Dallas Cowboys uniform and Peter is running around with this half-cracked helmet, and I'm running around just getting killed. In every video, I'm playing with some type of ball. I'm always playing."

One of Tebow's regrets is that he didn't play baseball his senior year of high school. Had he done so, he most likely would have been drafted by a major league baseball team.

As a homeschool student, Tebow put in the extra hours to earn his diploma ahead of senior students at Nease. Contrary to general belief, homeschooled students don't have a lighter class load than traditional students. Students who attend school are there from 8 a.m. to 3 p.m. However, education can be a full-time activity for the homeschooled. Lunch and dinner are often a time for quizzes. The extra work Tebow devoted to his high school studies allowed him to enroll at the University of Florida in the spring semester of 2006. Other kids his age would start their freshman year in the fall semester of 2006. But Tebow wanted to get a jump on his freshman teammates by participating in spring football.

"Which was the second hardest decision I've had to make because to be honest, I thought for most of my life that I would play baseball," Tebow said. "Because I was a lot better at it. I loved playing baseball."

A left-handed slugger, Tebow won his share of the annual home run derbies sponsored by his league. Had he been right-handed, who knows? Tebow might have developed into a power-hitting catcher or third baseman, where the throwing motion starts at the ear level—much like the way a quarterback is taught to throw.

But as a left-handed thrower, Tebow was limited in baseball to pitching, and playing the outfield and first base. What were Tim's thoughts about his much scrutinized throwing motion as a quarterback?

"That's 100 percent pitching," Tebow said. "The coaches

taught me that you break (your pitching hand from the glove) and you separate and you drop and then you follow through. And that's what I did first, before I started playing football. I pitched and developed my natural throwing motion before I started playing football. Everything I did in baseball was elongated because I was a pitcher, I was a first baseman, and I played outfield."

Tebow said the second toughest decision he's had to make in his sports career was giving up baseball in order to play college football. His most difficult decision was choosing to play college football for the University of Florida over Alabama.

Why did he ultimately choose football and not baseball?

"Baseball, even though I was better at it, the intensity just isn't there," Tebow said. "The passion is not the same."

Although Tebow is one of the most famous athletes in America, he has experienced the downside of fame. Fame means he can't go out to dinner without everyone in the restaurant staring at him. Fame for one person can trigger jealousy in another person. And jealousy can generate hurtful insults towards the famous person.

"Really, the only part about fame I like is it gives me a chance to have an impact on kids," Tebow said in front of his Broncos locker one day in 2011.

Generally, Tebow's message to kids is about faith, working hard, and being the best you can be. At some point, though, Tebow said he would like to spread his work to helping kids with dyslexia.

Tim Tebow was diagnosed as dyslexic. His dad and older brother, Robby, are also dyslexic. All three are "kinesthetic" learners.

"Rather than being auditory or visual, kinesthetic is learning by doing," Tebow said. "So if you say let's figure out how to work this TV, well if you just told me: 'hit this, this, and this,' I won't remember it as well. But if I go through it and do it, then I'll have it."

Pam Tebow helped her sons understand that dyslexia has nothing to do with intelligence. It just meant the Tebow men had to process learning differently than others.

"I don't think it's a handicap at all for me," Tebow said. "It's just about processing differently. It's

> Dyslexia is a learning disability a person is born with. It is a language problem that can hinder reading, writing, spelling, and even speaking. Dyslexia is not a sign of stupidity or laziness or the result of poor eyesight. Children and adults with dyslexia simply have a problem in their nervous system that causes their brains to process and interpret information in a different way.

something that interests me because kids learn so much differently. There's not a cookie-cutter way of 'Hey, this is how it is and based on these tests, this is your intelligence level.' No, that's silly. Some kids are brilliant in different ways. I feel bad when kids can't test well, that they're not looked at as smart."

Could dyslexia help explain why Tebow grew up to perform considerably better in games than in practice? Practice is about learning plays drawn up on diagrams and then repeated in practice. Practice is about following the plays by the book. Get the snap—one step, two steps, three steps back. Set up. Look. Throw.

There is a certain way, an exact way, to do it.

But in a game, plays don't often go according to how they were diagrammed. It is not about just thinking, but reacting. A play may be designed to throw a slant pattern to the left. But what happens if a safety moves into the area where the receiver is supposed to take the throw? At that point, the quarterback must think of something else to do. Not think. Do.

"I think in games it's just a fight," Tebow said. "And you do whatever you can to get past that line. Practice, it's about learning and improving. But the game is not thinking almost, it's playing, it's what you do in the backyard with your brothers."

One game the Tebow brothers played was three-man football. One brother would play quarterback, another would play receiver, and the third would cover the receiver as a defensive back.

The games with his brothers on the farm would eventually lead young Tim to the Denver Broncos as a first-round pick in the 2010 National Football League draft.

Chapter 3

First Round Shocker

Lonie Paxton was the long snapper on the Denver Broncos in 2010. A snapper's job is to hike the ball several yards back to the punter on punts, and to hold on extra points and field goals. Immediately, he must then block the charging giant defensive linemen intent on blocking the kick.

A tough job, but somebody's got to do it. Each year, Paxton held a first-round, draft-day bowling outing for charity in Colorado. About 15 Bronco players were there to bowl and also watch the first day of the 2010 NFL Draft on TV, which is the draft of eligible college football players, held that year over several days in New York City.

Kyle Orton and his wife Bridget attended the bowling party. It was fitting that Orton, the Bronco's starting quarterback, rolled the night's best score, a 268. He was the kind of guy his offensive teammates admired. Starting quarterback and a natural athlete, Orton was also the best golfer on the team. He was not a leader in a "rah-rah" way. But because teammates respected him, he set an example of leadership.

> NFL teams develop and improve their rosters in three ways: signing free-agent players, trading their players for players from other teams, and drafting college players who have declared themselves eligible for the NFL draft. The NFL draft is an annual three-day event in which all 32 teams take their turn selecting these players. There are seven rounds, which means about 245 players are chosen. The most highly regarded (and highest paid) players are selected in the first round.

The evening at the bowling center was winding down, with the first round of the draft reaching the 20th selection. The Broncos had traded back for the 22nd overall pick of the first round and selected Georgia Tech wide receiver Demaryius Thomas. There had been news reports the past day or so that Tebow was in the Broncos' sights as a potential pick late in the first round, but the selection of Thomas apparently ended that rumor.

Orton and his wife were leaving for home when they heard a commotion unrelated to crashing pins. The Broncos, after drafting Thomas with the 22nd overall pick, had made a trade with the Baltimore Ravens, acquiring the 25th pick as well. Orton watched on ESPN as his team selected Tim Tebow with that pick.

If Orton was irked, he didn't show it. But he must have realized that his days as the Broncos' starting quarterback were numbered.

The Broncos' selection of Tebow was stunning for several reasons. One, the team already had two established veteran quarterbacks in Orton and Brady Quinn, who the Broncos acquired a month earlier in a trade with the Cleveland Browns.

Until Tebow's arrival, Quinn had been arguably the NFL's most popular young quarterback. Quinn was a superb quarterback at Notre Dame and a first-round draft choice of the Cleveland Browns in 2007.

Although Tebow's first-round selection by the Broncos was not totally unexpected, it sent a seismic tremor throughout the NFL Draft. The non-stop draft coverage by ESPN and the NFL Network became non-stop coverage of Tebow and the Broncos.

The Denver Post had reported the night before the draft that the Broncos might select Tebow. Several NFL teams had dropped hints to Tebow's agent Jimmy Sexton that they might choose the quarterback in the second or third rounds and groom him for a starting role in future seasons.

Historically, Notre Dame's program was vital in building the overall popularity of college football beginning with the era of legendary coach Knute Rockne from 1918 to 1930. Through its last national championship under Coach Lou Holtz in 1988, the Fighting Irish won 13 national titles and produced 7 Heisman Trophy winners, the most in college football in that time span. Notre Dame had come off disappointing 5–7 and 6–6 seasons in 2003–04 when the school hired Charlie Weis as head coach. With Brady Quinn at quarterback, Weis led Notre Dame to 9–3 and 10–3 seasons in 2005–06. The year after Quinn left, though, Notre Dame and Weis slipped to 3–9.

Only the Broncos, however, were willing to draft him so highly in the first round. Head coach Josh McDaniels and general manager Brian Xanders had visited with University of Texas quarterback Colt McCoy on the Monday before the Draft, Thomas on Tuesday in Georgia, and Tebow later that day in Florida. Between McCoy and Tebow, McDaniels and Xanders came away far more impressed with the Florida lefty.

The Broncos' selection of Tebow only heightened the scrutiny of the Heisman Trophy winner. Bashing the pick became almost a daily event.

The notion that Tebow could not succeed as an every-down NFL quarterback intensified during Senior Bowl week in late January. The top college seniors gather each year in Mobile, Alabama for practices and an all-star exhibition game. Every team sends its coaches, scouts, and personnel staff to evaluate which players have the talent to play in the NFL.

The week of practice generates the most scouting interest. In fact, most of the coaches and staff leave before the actual game is played.

The Senior Bowl is not well-suited for a player of Tebow's talents. He has always been a gamer, and not always a good practice player.

Practice is about running the plays as they're drawn up in the playbook. Tebow is not a follow-the-diagram kind of quarterback. It's when the play breaks down that Tebow showcases his incredible improvisational skills.

Tebow's freelancing style of play is one reason it was so shocking that Denver drafted him in the first place. Coach McDaniels ran an extremely systematic offense. Pass patterns were precise with one or two receivers serving as decoys to set up the primary receiver to make the catch. Tebow is the quintessential unsystematic quarterback. There is far more exhilarating chaos than precision in his game.

So, why did McDaniels and Xanders fly to Florida to work out Tebow two days before the draft? One reason was sheer boldness. Since McDaniels became the Broncos' head coach in January 2009, he had proved to be nothing if not bold. He traded quarterback Jay Cutler and receiver

Jay Cutler became the Chicago Bears' starting quarterback, but originally he was the Broncos' first-round draft pick, No. 11 overall, in 2006. When the coach who drafted him, Mike Shanahan, was fired after the 2008 season, Cutler was irate. He immediately asked to be traded. When the Broncos replaced Shanahan as coach with McDaniels, a 32-year-old offensive coordinator from New England, Cutler repeated his trade demand because it meant Jeremy Bates, the current Broncos' 32-year-old offensive coordinator, would not be retained. No NFL staff has room for two young offensive coordinators when one is rare. Cutler calmed down until he learned that McDaniels had investigated a trade that would have reunited him with New England quarterback Matt Cassel. Cutler and McDaniels could never resolve their differences and the saga became known as "McJaygate." Cutler was traded to the Bears, along with a fifth-round draft pick, in exchange for Orton, two first-round draft picks and a third-round pick.

Brandon Marshall, two young stars coming off Pro Bowl appearances, because of personality conflicts. If he was bold enough to trade those two stars, McDaniels was bold enough to draft Tebow.

Tebow made sense for the Broncos because McDaniels insisted his quarterbacks must be proven winners. McDaniels, remember, was raised in the New England Patriots' system. He was an assistant coach when the Pats won Super Bowls in 2001, 2003, and 2004. He was New England's offensive coordinator in 2007, when the Pats set a still-standing scoring record and reached the Super Bowl with an undefeated record.

McDaniels was also the Pats' offensive coordinator in 2008 when star quarterback Tom Brady suffered a season-ending knee injury in the first quarter of the first game of the season. Yet, backup Matt Cassel, who had not started since high school, guided New England to an 11–5 record.

The other attribute McDaniels looked for in a quarterback was size, at least 6 foot, 3 inches tall. At that height, a quarterback can stand tall in the pocket from the shotgun formation and peer over the massive offensive and defensive linemen to complete passes.

Tebow fit this mold. He was 6 foot, 2⅝-inches tall. And as for winning, has there ever been a quarterback from a

The 2007 New England Patriots nearly rewrote the record book. They finished the regular season 16–0—the first NFL team since the 1972 Miami Dolphins to go undefeated in the regular season. But the Dolphins, who went 14–0 during the regular season and finished 17–0 after winning Super Bowl VII, remained the league's only unbeaten team. The Pats were 18–0 before losing the Super Bowl to the New York Giants, 17–14 on a last-minute touchdown pass from Giants' quarterback Eli Manning to Plaxico Burress.

top 5 college program who won more big games than Tebow?

Coach McDaniels wanted all his players, not just quarterbacks, to be high on character and intelligence. Tebow's All-American persona rated him as the consensus No. 1 character guy to come along in the draft in years.

As for intelligence, Tebow impressed McDaniels and Xanders with the results of his "board" test. In a board test, an NFL coach will ask a player to draw up offense or defense on an erasable white board. Tebow diagrammed various defensive coverages, blitzes, and alignments on the board. He was asked how he would "check out" or change play calls when he saw how defenses would attack.

"He aced it," Xanders said. "He was incredible on the board."

As a passer, Tebow was a project. But McDaniels, and his brother Ben, the Broncos' quarterbacks coach in 2010, were confident they could develop Tebow into an efficient passer.

McDaniels' confidence was bolstered by the fact that under his direct coaching, Tom Brady threw for a still-standing NFL record 50 touchdowns in 2007. McDaniels helped Matt Cassel engineer an 11–5 record for the Pats while subbing for the injured Brady in 2008.

Guiding Matt Cassel and the Patriots to 11 wins in 2008 was a remarkable coaching feat because Cassel had never started a game in college at quarterback. At Southern Cal, Cassel played behind two Heisman Trophy winners. First Carson Palmer, who won the Heisman in 2002, and then Matt Leinart, who won it in 2004. Nevertheless, Patriots scout Matt Russell was impressed by Cassel's performance at his Pro Day workout before the draft and convinced his boss, Coach Bill Belichick, to select the backup quarterback in the seventh round of the 2005 draft. After the 2008 season, with Brady returning as the starter, the Pats traded Cassel to the Kansas City Chiefs.

McDaniels also helped Orton to his career-best season in 2009. Before joining the Broncos, Orton had never thrown for more than 3,000 yards in his two seasons with the Chicago Bears, where he had 30 touchdown passes against 27 interceptions. In 2009 and 2010 with the Broncos, Orton threw for 3,802 yards one year and 3,653 yards the next. He had 41 combined TD passes against 21 interceptions.

So, McDaniels had a well-deserved reputation for developing quarterbacks. But McDaniels would be considered a coaching genius if he could turn Tebow into an efficient passer.

Tebow could develop as a rookie by watching Orton from the sidelines during games. But McDaniels also thought Tebow could be used on a few plays each game as a running quarterback in the so-called "Wildcat" formation. In 2009, the Broncos had struggled to pick up first downs, rushing on third-and-1 and fourth-and-1 situations.

The case for the Broncos selecting Tebow was made. Now, they had to land him.

Executing the plan was a different matter. No one considered Tebow worthy of a top 15 pick, and the Broncos started the draft with the No. 11 selection. The Broncos, therefore, would have to either trade back from their No. 11 overall spot in the draft's first round, or up from their No. 43 spot in the second round.

As it turned out, they did both. They traded back twice in the first round in return for extra picks. They then took advantage of the extra picks they accumulated to package three of them together (one in the second round, another in the third round, and another in the fourth) and trade up to Baltimore's spot at No. 25.

Once NFL commissioner Roger Goodell announced the

Broncos' selection of Tebow, the buzz of draft day exploded into a roar.

Like always with Tebow, the commotion was mixed. Critics shook their heads at McDaniels. This brash young coach was gaining a reputation, fair or not, of possessing a large ego. He's the same guy who thought his system was more important than a 24-year-old Pro Bowl quarterback in Jay Cutler. And now McDaniels thinks he's such a hot-shot coach he can fix all things that are wrong with Tebow?

Having played almost exclusively from the shotgun formation at Florida, Tebow was unfamiliar with taking three, five, or seven step drops from center to the pocket. That drop must be made while scanning the defense, figuring out quickly where the open receiver will be, and then delivering on time.

It's more difficult than it appears. And it was an extremely difficult exercise for Tebow to perform during the Senior Bowl practices. He was a mechanical mess in Mobile. Besides his inefficient footwork, Tebow would hold the ball extremely low before delivering his throw. The result was a long arm swing on his delivery, much closer to a baseball pitch than the quick release required of NFL quarterbacks.

Tebow tried to deliver the ball more quickly in Mobile, but as he did, his accuracy suffered. His poor Senior Bowl workouts figured to either drop his stock from the first round to at least the third, or it would cause teams to think of him as an H-back, as some experts had suggested. Tebow, though, would have none of that. He would only play quarterback in the pros.

"You only need one team to believe," he told *The Denver Post*'s Jeff Legwold.

That team would be the Broncos.

Although he was a Heisman Trophy winner and a finalist two other times, and guided Florida to two national titles, few NFL experts thought Tebow had the passing skills to succeed as an NFL quarterback.

He was considered a great football player—not a great quarterback.

But Coach McDaniels loved Tebow's athleticism, intelligence, competitiveness, and intangible leadership qualities. He thought he could teach Tebow how to pass.

By the time Tebow was given a serious chance to justify McDaniels' decision, though, the coach was gone. McDaniels was fired with four games left in Tebow's 2010 rookie season. Not only had the Broncos posted an embarrassing 3–9 record through the first 12 games of McDaniels' second season, the coach was sanctioned by the league for his role in covering up an illicit videotaping incident by a member of the team's video department, a person he had hired.

That video scandal would tarnish the otherwise proud Broncos' reputation as one of the classiest organizations in the league. Owner Pat Bowlen and his right-hand man Joe Ellis felt it was time for the organization to change football leaders.

Eventually, McDaniels' firing would come back to haunt Tebow. McDaniels was the coach who most believed in Tebow, whatever his flaws as a passer. With McDaniels gone, the Broncos' new football administration headed by John Elway and John Fox eventually brought in all-time great Peyton Manning as quarterback, an acquisition that in turn led Tebow to the New York Jets.

But before Elway and Fox gave up on Tebow, they prospered from him. Jump ahead to Tebow's second season. More specifically, the game played on Nov. 27, 2011, when the Broncos defeated their AFC West rival San Diego Chargers in overtime. The win was the fourth in a row since Tebow replaced Orton as the starter. The win epitomized McDaniels' mindset in drafting Tebow so highly.

Wrote Mike Klis in his game story of the Broncos' overtime win in San Diego for *The Denver Post*:

SAN DIEGO – This was why the Broncos drafted Tim Tebow in the first round. It was for this game, against this opponent, to outplay, if not necessarily outpass, the Broncos' primary nemesis, Philip Rivers.

If the Broncos were going to win the Super Bowl for the first time since the 1998 season, they would first have to win the AFC West.

For the better part of the past seven years, the Chargers were considered the division's team to beat. Going on the past six seasons, Rivers was considered the best quarterback in the division.

In a remarkably hard-fought, muscle-wearing rival matchup that took nearly a full extra quarter to decide, Tebow and the Broncos beat Rivers and the Chargers 16–13 in overtime on a warm Sunday afternoon at Qualcomm Stadium.

Any chance Broncos fans can start to realize not everything about the abbreviated Josh McDaniels era in Denver was bad?

"I'm happy we have him," coach John Fox said of Tebow.

As the Broncos' first-year coach, Fox is the beneficiary of McDaniels' controversial choice with the No. 25 pick in the 2010 draft.

Against the Chargers, Tebow accounted for 210 total yards with 143 yards passing and 67 yards rushing— on a whopping 22 carries, many off the much-discussed read option that Fox implemented four games—and four wins— ago. Rivers accounted for 189 total yards with 188 yards passing and 1 yard rushing.

Just like the Broncos drew it up.

It was McDaniels who thought Tebow could give the Broncos a counter to Rivers in the annual twice-a-year meetings for AFC West supremacy. It wasn't just that Rivers has always been an elite quarterback. What also struck McDaniels about Rivers is his fiery competitiveness.

The Broncos needed to counter that uber competitiveness. As Tebow rallied the Broncos to victory despite deficits of 15–0 with three minutes remaining at Miami two months ago, 24–14 midway through the third quarter at Oakland, 13–10 inside the two-minute warning against the New York Jets, and 13–10 again Sunday with less than two minutes remaining in regulation against the Chargers, is there any question about Tebow's competitiveness?

Said Brian Xanders, the Denver general manager who worked alongside McDaniels, during the 2010 draft: "We looked at him as, had a great winning record at Florida. He had competitive toughness. High-end production in the running game and passing game in college. We knew he had to improve in the passing game, but he had a lot of traits we were looking for."

Tebow doesn't get it done by conventional NFL quarterback methods. But he gets it done. The Broncos have won five of the six games he has started this year and are 6–5, in position to reach the AFC playoffs for the first time since 2005. The Broncos trail the 7–4 Oakland Raiders by one game in the AFC West and the 7–4 Cincinnati Bengals by one game for an AFC wild card.

Afterward, a shiner on his right cheek, Tebow was collecting his postgame meal near the buses when Rivers walked by. "Good job, Tim," he said.

Tebow was winning in the NFL with the same style he had won in his four years at the University of Florida.

Chapter 4

Another Tebow Upset

Tim Tebow did not play quarterback as a freshman in high school. After transferring to another high school, his team lost five of his last six games as a sophomore. Still, he was one of the most heavily recruited quarterbacks in the country during his junior and senior seasons at Ponte Vedra Beach Nease High School, located about 18 miles southeast of Jacksonville, Fla.

No matter how unknown the player, Division I college football recruiters will find the talent. Tebow actually received his first two recruitment letters, from Louisville and Ohio State, during his sophomore year in high school. As a junior and senior, he took numerous "unofficial" visits to all of the top football powers—Alabama, LSU, Clemson, Georgia, Florida State, Tennessee, Maryland, Miami, Ohio State, Michigan, USC, Notre Dame, and Florida.

In an "unofficial" visit, the recruit or someone from the recruit's party pays for the trip. In Tebow's case, it was his father. There is no limit to the number of unofficial visits a recruit can make. Tebow grew up a college football junkie so it was hardly a chore for him to spend his weekends attending college football games across the South. He took three "unofficial" visits to Alabama alone.

Each recruit is also allotted five "official" visits, when the college program pays for the trip and accommodations. While there are exceptions to any rule, a recruit will almost always choose from one of the colleges in which he officially visited. The five college programs who made the official visit list for Tebow were Alabama, Florida, USC, Michigan, and LSU.

Notre Dame was eliminated because it was a bone-chilling cold the day Tebow saw the Fighting Irish face Boston College in South Bend, Ind. Georgia passed on Tebow after the Bulldogs received a commitment from another hot prospect, Matthew Stafford. Tebow was cool to Tennessee because during an unofficial visit his junior year, the Volunteers' coaching staff fawned over senior quarterback recruit Jonathan Crompton.

As Homer Simpson might say: Doh!

Southern Cal (USC) had little chance to land Tebow because of its West Coast location. The campus was too far from Tebow's home and family in Jacksonville. Since entering the NFL, Tebow meets with various family members after every game, home and road. During his two years with the Denver Broncos, Tebow shared his house with his two brothers, Robby and Peter. Family is everything to Tim Tebow. Playing for the USC Trojans would essentially mean playing without family. The USC coach, Pete Carroll, could out-recruit just about anyone in the country, but there was no pitch that could persuade Tebow to leave his family behind.

Crompton basically became a one-year starter for Tennessee, leading the Vols to a 7–6 record as a senior. He did have 27 TD passes against 13 interceptions; impressive enough to become a fifth round pick of the Washington Redskins in 2010—the same draft in which Tebow was taken in the first round by the Broncos. Crompton has yet to attempt an NFL pass.

Stafford was a full-time starter as a sophomore and junior at Georgia, leading the Bulldogs to a 21–5 record in those two years. He was the No. 1 overall selection of the Detroit Lions in the 2009 draft and had a breakout year in 2011, when he threw for 5,039 yards and 41 touchdowns while leading Detroit to its first playoff appearance in 12 seasons.

In the end, Tebow's decision came down to two schools: Alabama, whose coach was Mike Shula, and Florida, coached by Urban Meyer. Meyer's successful spread offense appealed to Tebow.

Despite the intensity of the sports rivalry between Florida and Alabama, Tebow, although considered a Floridian, leaned toward the Crimson Tide. Alabama's recruiting process was simply the "gold standard" by which all other programs were measured. 'Bama fans would make the 8½-hour road trip to attend Tebow's high school games in the Jacksonville area.

During his official visit to the Tuscaloosa, Ala. campus, Tebow was invited to run out of the tunnel with the Crimson Tide players before the game. He saw a sign that read: STABLER, NAMATH, TEBOW. Having his name on a sign with two all-time great Alabama quarterbacks was humbling. On the sideline, Tebow was introduced to legendary NFL coach Don Shula, father of the Alabama coach.

No two players brought more flair to the NFL quarterback position in the 1960s and 70s than "Broadway" Joe Namath and Kenny "The Snake" Stabler. This was in contrast to their college background because each played for legendary coach Bear Bryant at Alabama. Bryant was an old-school, by-the-book disciplinarian. Namath led the Tide to the 1964 national championship and posted a 29–4 record during his three years as a starter (1962–64). Stabler was 19–2–1 in his two 'Bama (1966–67), including 11–0 in 1966 when the AP and coaches poll nevertheless awarded 9–0–1 Notre Dame the national championship.

Namath went on to lead the New York Jets of the upstart American Football League to a historic win in Super Bowl III following the 1968 season, and Stabler quarterbacked the Oakland Raiders to the Super Bowl XI title following the 1976 season.

The University of Florida, though, is where Tebow's parents and his sister Katie graduated. His brother Peter was also attending Florida the year Tim was a senior in high school when the recruiting process was at its most intense.

As a youth, Tebow was a huge Florida fan. His bedroom was plastered with posters of Gators players and adorned with blue and orange memorabilia, the official colors of the school.

Asked to name their favorite football player, most kids would probably name a top NFL quarterback such as Tom Brady, Peyton Manning, or Aaron Rodgers. But when Tebow was a kid, he was different. He had many favorites, but if he had to pick one, it would probably be Danny Wuerffel. Although he failed as a pro quarterback, as a college player, Wuerffel led the Florida Gators to four consecutive Southeast Conference (SEC) titles. This was a feat that not even the highly decorated Tebow could later top. In 1996, when Tebow was at the impressionable age of 9, Wuerffel won the Heisman Trophy. Wuerffel also shares Tebow's Christian values. Wuerffel once spoke at a church where afterwards, a young Tim Tebow stood in line for well more than an hour to get his autograph.

On December 10, 2005, Tebow led his underdog Ponte Verde Beach Nease team to the Florida Class 4A state title with a 44–37 win again two-time defending champion Seffner Armwood. Led? How about carried. His performance in this state championship game will long be remembered and recounted. Tebow completed 18 of 27 passes for 237 yards and four touchdowns. He also rushed for 153 yards and two more touchdowns. His six total touchdowns, a state record, accounted for 41 points. As for the other three points, on a short field goal, Tebow set that up with a 70-yard run.

But wait—there's more. Tebow's Panthers were ahead 34–15 at halftime and 41–22 after three quarters, but Seffner Armwood stormed back to outscore Nease, 15–3 in the fourth quarter. Not only had the score closed to 44–37, Armwood had recovered the onside kick with 1:12 left in the game.

Nease was in trouble. Tebow convinced his coach, Craig Howard, to let him play nose guard on defense. Nose guard? That's a position usually reserved for the largest member of the team. Although a quarterback, Tebow was built like a defensive high school lineman—6-foot, 2-inches, 225 pounds. Seffner Armwood lost 7 yards on its next four plays, and Nease had won the state championship.

Three days later, Tebow decided where he would play college football. The announcement would be made at a press conference held at Nease's school auditorium. In those three days between the biggest win of his life, and the biggest decision of his life, Tebow had narrowed his choices to Alabama and Florida.

Florida recruiters met with him on December 11, the afternoon after the state championship game. That night, it was the LSU recruiters turn. On the next day, Tebow spent 14 hours with the Alabama contingent.

LSU wound up his third choice. Tebow loved the college atmosphere in Baton Rouge, La., but he could never move the Tigers ahead of the Crimson Tide or Gators.

On the morning of December 13, decision day, Tebow was still torn between Alabama and Florida. Tebow's autobiography discusses how he prayed to the Lord for guidance, but the answer would not come. Tebow then shared a profound lesson for people of faith.

"People often seem to think that when you're following the Lord and trying to do His will, your path will always be clear, the decisions smooth and easy, and life will be lived happily ever after," Tebow wrote. "Sometimes that may be true but I've found that more often it's not."

Seven years later, as Tebow sat in the Broncos' cafeteria in January 2012, his memories of the difficulty of choosing between Florida and Alabama were still vivid.

"That definitely was the hardest decision I ever made in my life," Tebow said. "I was agonizing, sweating. It was a miserable time. It was supposed to be a great day for me. It was one of the worst."

The auditorium was packed. Tebow's decision was such an enormous event that David Garrard, who had just replaced the injured Byron Leftwich as the Jacksonville Jaguars starting quarterback, was in the audience.

"Finally, I asked my dad, 'Dad, where do you think I should go?' Tebow said. "Dad said, 'Who's the one person you want to play for?' I loved coach Shula, loved coach Meyer. I told him: I don't know, probably coach Meyer.

"So I picked up the phone and I called coach Shula and he could tell I was crying because I thought I was going to Alabama since I was a freshman. I loved the passion of Alabama because I felt like that was my passion. And the coaches, and the hugs, and the sweet tea, and the people. It felt like home to me.

"But then Urban, his passion and his love for the game and the way he believed in me and I believed in what he was doing, and I was thinking: 'There's something special with him.'"

Urban Meyer had won arguably the most intense individual recruiting battle in decades. Tebow would play the next four years in Gainesville, home of the Florida Gators.

Tebow made his decision just three days after winning the state high school championship because he wanted to enroll early at college. An advantage of homeschooling was that Tebow could work ahead. He earned his high school diploma in December 2005. This allowed him to get a jump on his freshman teammates by enrolling at Florida in the spring of 2006. While the other Gator recruits were finishing high school, Tebow was participating in Florida's spring practice.

All the visits to college campuses during his junior and

senior years in high school had taught Tebow the value of spring practice as it relates to playing time the following fall—when it counts.

Incoming freshman Tebow led his team past senior-to-be Chris Leak's team in the Gators' spring intrasquad scrimmage. Still, Leak would be the starter at quarterback in 2006 with Tebow serving as the backup. He would enter the game on short yardage and goal-to-go plays. Tebow's freshman year at Florida brought the famous jump pass and a national championship.

Although Tebow completed just 22 passes (out of 33 attempts) that first year, five were for touchdowns. He also rushed for eight touchdowns and became easily the most talked-about second-string quarterback in the country.

His sophomore season at Florida was bittersweet. Bitter results as a team; sweet production as an individual. On the plus side, he became the Gators' starting quarterback for the first time. He also became the first-ever sophomore in college history to win the Heisman Trophy.

The down side to his sophomore season was that after a 4–0 start, the Gators finished 9–4, including a 41–35 loss to Michigan in their season-ending bowl game. It was the Gators' worst won-loss record during the Tebow era.

Still, Heisman voters could not ignore Tebow's spectacular individual achievements. Never before had college football seen a player like him, a quarterback who was both a determined runner and—despite what NFL critics would later say of him—an accurate and productive passer.

In a win at Mississippi, Tebow threw 34 passes for 261 yards and two touchdowns and rushed an astounding 27 times for 166 yards and another two touchdowns—an incredible 61 touches in a 30–24 win.

One of the greatest single-game performances in years came at a time—game 4 of the season on Sept. 22, 2007—when Heisman voters start setting their initial ballots. And if any voters were still unsure, there was Tebow's seven-touchdown, 424-yard passing-and-rushing performance in a 51–31 win against South Carolina on Nov. 11.

Tebow finished his sophomore season with Heisman-caliber credentials—32 touchdown passes against just six interceptions for 3,286 yards on a 66.9 completion rate, plus 895 yards rushing including another 23 touchdowns that set an NCAA record among quarterbacks.

The combined 55 touchdowns and 4,181 yards were unprecedented single-season numbers. No other college player had passed and rushed for at least 20 touchdowns in the same season.

> Only 18 of 120 NCAA Division I football teams scored at least 55 touchdowns, which Tebow personally accounted for in the 2007 season. And 19 NCAA Division I teams—including Notre Dame, Miami of Florida, and Iowa—had fewer than Tebow's 4,181 yards in total offense. Statistically, Tebow was clearly a one-man team in 2007.

Tebow's junior season became a season unto itself. It brought hopes of Florida's first-ever undefeated season. It brought Tebow a third-place finish in the Heisman Trophy ratings even though he had the most first-place votes. And it brought Florida its second national title in Tebow's first three years at the school.

Impressive as all those accomplishments may have been for just about any other football star, Tim Tebow was the star of stars. Somehow, some way, he manages to do something even more captivating, even more memorable than any previous mortal feats. Something that goes beyond even the level where only the brightest stars can reach.

The legend of Tebow soared to even greater heights with what is now known throughout college football as "The Promise."

Chapter 5

"The Promise"

To parents, "promise" is talent shown by their son scoring a winning touchdown in pee-wee football. To that child, a "promise" may be the ice cream cone his father promised to him in scoring that touchdown. But mention "The Promise" to fans of University of Florida football, and Gator Nation will have the same reaction. In fact, many fans can probably recite Tim Tebow's famous pledge word-for-word.

"The Promise" was the emotional speech of Florida quarterback Tim Tebow at his press conference following the Gators' 31–30 upset loss to Ole Miss early in the 2008 football season. It had a lasting impact on everyone, particularly on Tebow's own teammates. A teammate commented that his words revealed as much about Tim Tebow, the man, as the football player.

> Enthusiastic supporters of a sports team are often referred to as "Nation." Boston Red Sox fans call themselves "Red Sox Nation." Florida Gator fans are known as "Gator Nation."

What made "The Promise" perhaps the greatest football speech since Coach Knute Rockne motivated his Notre Dame football team to "Win one for the Gipper!" is that Tebow's would prove to be accurate at the end of the long 2008 season. His claim was bold, even brash, but he would back up his words with action.

And wins. Victory after victory. Tebow would keep winning until he led the Gators to the most important college win of all to cap the 2008 season.

*George Gipp was the first All-American football player at Notre Dame. Near the end of his final season in 1920, he contracted strep throat which led to pneumonia and an infection. Without the benefit of modern medicine, Gipp was on his death bed when he supposedly said to his coach Knute Rockne: "Rock, when the team is up against it, when things are wrong and the breaks are beating the boys, ask them to go in there with all they've got and win just one for the Gipper." As the story goes, it wasn't until eight years later, at halftime against a strong Army team, that coach Rockne told his Notre Dame players to "win one for the Gipper." The Irish rallied in the second half to beat Army, 12–6.

To fully understand why Tebow's "Promise" speech became so famous, it is important to relate the events that led up to the speech. In his freshman year at Florida, Tebow was the second-string quarterback to senior starter Chris Leak. Tebow would come off the bench on short-yardage and goal-line plays, and he often helped the Gators' offense by either picking up first

In short-yardage plays, an offense only needs three yards or fewer for a first down. A team earns a first down each time it travels 10 yards. The team gets four downs to go those 10 yards. Sometimes, an offense will have third down and 2 yards to go for a first down. Football announcers will usually call this situation: Third-and-2. The first number indicates the down. The second number indicates the yardage needed for a first down.

*In the movie "Knute Rockne: All-American," the role of George Gipp was played by Ronald Reagan, who would later become the President of the United States.

downs to help sustain offensive drives, or by finishing them off with touchdowns.

A major reason for Tebow's success in short-yardage plays was his threat to run or pass. The defense was unsure what he would do on any particular play and that moment's hesitation was just enough for Tebow to take advantage.

Also helping Tebow was the "jump pass" which he made famous in his freshman season at Florida. The jump pass was frequently used near the goal line. Tebow would take the snap from the shotgun position, which means he was lined up about 5 yards behind the center. He would run toward the line of scrimmage. To the defense, it looked like Tebow was keeping the ball to run. Defenders would charge ahead to stop him. Tebow would then stop before the line of scrimmage, leap into the air, and throw a short pass, usually to a wide-open receiver! (Tebow had to stop before the line of scrimmage before making the jump pass. An illegal forward pass penalty is called if the passer is beyond the line of scrimmage when the throw is made.)

Chris Leak was the starting Gator quarterback in 2006. But Tebow's jump passes were the center of attention, often replayed on TV nationally on ESPN's Sportscenter. Add his exuberant, youthful reaction to scoring touchdowns and soon Tebow and his "jump pass" became a hot topic around the country's playgrounds and offices.

As a freshman, Tebow attempted just 33 passes, but he completed 22 (67 percent) for 358 yards and five touchdowns. He also rushed the ball 89 times for 469 yards (a 5.3 yard per carry average) and eight more touchdowns. There aren't many second-string quarterbacks at any level accounting for 13 touchdowns in a season, much less at the NCAA national championship level.

For that's what the Gators became in 2006, Tebow's freshman season: national champs. The team went 13–1 that year and trounced Ohio State in the BCS Championship Game, 41–14.

The BCS is short for Bowl Championship Series. Division I football is the only sport and division that does not award its champion through an elimination tournament. Instead, the BCS is a selection system formed in 1998 that creates five major bowl games for what is considered the top 10 ranked teams in the country. The top two-ranked teams play in the BCS Championship. However, in June 2012 NCAA presidents adopted a 4 team division I playoff starting with the 2014 season.

After the Gators won the 2006 national championship, many seniors ran out of college eligibility and star underclassmen turned professional. Leak was among those who left, which meant Tebow, a sophomore, became the Gators' full-time starting quarterback in 2007. Tebow had a spectacular season, passing for 32 touchdowns against just six interceptions, while rushing for 23 touchdowns. Think about that again—55 touchdowns from one player in a single season!

Tebow's season was so spectacular, he was the first sophomore awarded the Heisman Trophy* as college football's most outstanding player.

As rewarding as

Winning this prestigious award has been no guarantee for success at the professional (NFL) level. In fact, the first winner, Berwanger, who was drafted by the Chicago Bears, never played professionally. More recently, Florida State's Charlie Ward (1993) and Oklahoma's Jason White (2003) never played in the NFL.

Tebow's sophomore season was for him personally, it was a disappointment to the team, which finished 9–4, including a 41–35 loss to Michigan in the season-ending Capital One

*The Heisman Trophy was first awarded to college football's best player in 1935. Running back Jay Berwanger of the University of Chicago was the first recipient.

Bowl. Nine wins and four losses would be the worst record Tebow endured in his four seasons at Florida.

Motivated by the disappointing 2007 season, Tebow not only trained harder than he ever did before—if that is possible given his dedicated workout regimen—he made sure his teammates followed him to the weight room and practice field for extra passing sessions, running, and conditioning. The goal Tebow and the Gators set for 2008 was not just a national championship, but Florida's first undefeated season.

At first, it looked like Florida would win every game, easily. The Gators opened the season by routing Hawaii, 56–10, then whipping in-state rival Miami, 26–3, before going to hostile territory in Knoxville, Tenn. and destroying the Tennessee Vols, 30–6. The Gators were not only 3–0; they had outscored three quality opponents by a combined score of 112–19.

Tebow was intent on getting his teammates involved early. He realized from his sophomore season that playing well enough to win the Heisman Trophy as the best individual player in the country did not necessarily mean the team would win the national championship. The other players had to produce as well. While his overall yardage totals were relatively modest by his standards, he did have five touchdown passes and no interceptions in the Gators' 3–0 start.

Game 4 figured to be another win as the Gators played Mississippi at Florida's stadium affectionately known as "The Swamp." The Ole Miss Rebels entered the game with a mediocre 2–2 record.

But for this one September Saturday afternoon the game went Ole Miss's way just enough to hang on for a 31–30 win. It seemed the ease of the Gators' victories in their first three games, plus a 17–7 halftime lead against the Rebels, had made Florida too overconfident.

Down 31–24 with about 5 minutes remaining in the game, Tebow did try to arouse his team from its sluggish play. He led Florida down the field for a game-tying touchdown. Or so the Gators figured. But after Florida's sensational multipurpose threat Percy Harvin scored on a 15-yard touchdown run to narrow the score to 31–30, the extra point kick was blocked. Ole Miss pulled off the most stunning upset of the college season thanks to that missed extra point. In defeat, Tebow was sensational on the field but very upset in the postgame locker room. He completed 24 of 38 passes for 319 yards and one touchdown with no interceptions. He also rushed for two touchdowns.

Not surprisingly, no one in the Gators' home locker room took the defeat harder than Tebow. He sat silently and somberly in front of his locker for 45 minutes. Tebow did not want to talk to waiting reporters, but also knew athletes must be held accountable for their play both in victory and defeat. Especially in defeat. He showered slowly and took even more time to dress, even if all he wore to the game that day were jeans and a black T-shirt.

As Tebow finally entered the media room and stood behind the podium that

When the Gators played on the road, players and coaches had to wear suits and ties on the team bus and plane. They represented their school, and coach Urban Meyer wanted to make sure the University of Florida was shown in the best possible manner. At home, the dress code was more casual.

had a single microphone at its center, he still didn't know what he wanted to say. He offered a quick prayer and what followed was unrehearsed and straight from his heart. It may have been corny, Hollywood movie stuff—much like the "win one for the Gipper" speech was in Knute Rockne: All-American.

But his words were also 100 percent genuine Tebow:

"I just want to say one thing. To the fans and everybody in Gator Nation, I'm sorry. I'm extremely sorry. We were hoping for an undefeated season... But I promise you one thing ...You will never see any player in the entire country play as hard as I will

Tebow looks for an open receiver as quarterback for his college football team, the Florida Gators.

Tebow runs the ball.

Diving for the end zone, Tebow scores a touchdown for the Gators.

As a college football player, Tim Tebow set a number of records for schools in the Southeastern Conference.

Tim Tebow greets the fans as a Denver Bronco.

Scoring his first NFL touchdown.

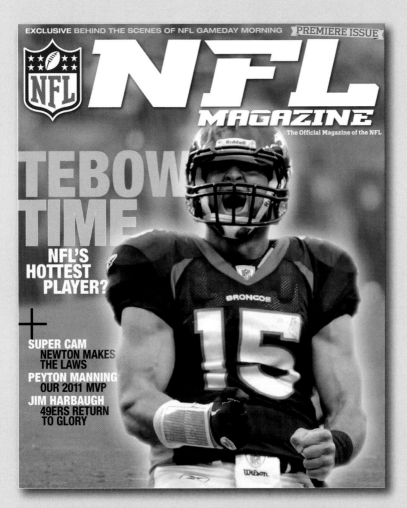

NFL
MAGAZINE
The Official Magazine of the NFL

TEBOW TIME
NFL'S HOTTEST PLAYER?

+

SUPER CAM
NEWTON MAKES THE LAWS

PEYTON MANNING
OUR 2011 MVP

JIM HARBAUGH
49ERS RETURN TO GLORY

Tebowmania strikes the NFL!

Tebowing during a game.

Much of Tebow's charitable work is with children.

Tebow prepares for the next phase of his career with the New York Jets.

play the rest of the season. And you will never see someone push the rest of the team as hard as I will push everybody the rest of the season, and you will never see a team play harder than we will the rest of this season. God Bless."

The next week, the Gators destroyed Arkansas in Fayetteville, 38–7. LSU was next. The Tigers picked a bad time to play Tebow and the Gators. LSU was crushed 51–21. Kentucky had no chance. The Wildcats were obliterated, 63–5. Yes, 63–5!

In the Georgia–Florida Football Classic that is played in the hardly neutral site of Jacksonville (It's not neutral because Jacksonville is Tebow's hometown); the Bulldogs had no chance, losing 49–10. Vandy was walloped 42–14.

Steve Spurrier, who was once a successful head coach at the University of Florida, leading the Gators to a national championship in the 1996 season, was next on the schedule. Spurrier was now coaching South Carolina and his former team trounced his Gamecocks, 56–6. The Citadel picked the wrong week to schedule a game at Florida. Tebow completed 9 of 11 passes for a whopping 201 yards and three touchdowns in a 70–19 win. There's another score worth repeating: 70–19. Florida State–the Gators' fiercest rival—was hammered 45–10.

There were eight consecutive wins since "The Promise," and an 8–0 record by a combined score of 414–92—an average score of 52–12! And it could have been worse had coach Meyer not made sure his reserves got some well-deserved playing time in the fourth quarter of those blowout victories.

The Gators play in the Southeastern Conference (SEC), usually against the strongest teams in college football. In the SEC championship, Number 1 ranked Alabama could not contain the determined Tebow and the Gators. The Crimson Tide was dominated, 31–20.

Despite the loss to Ole Miss, Tebow had his best college season. He threw 30 touchdowns against just four interceptions—unheard of passing numbers. Not only did he lead the Gators to a 12–1 record, but the average score in those 13 games was 45–13.

Florida was arguably one of the best college football teams of all time, given their stiff competition within the SEC.

Yet, Heisman Trophy voters were not convinced Tebow deserved to be awarded the trophy as college football's best player for a second consecutive season. Tebow has said he thought he was more deserving of the Heisman Trophy in his junior season. As a sophomore, he was a fresh story exploding on the scene. As a junior, Tebow's play, while even better than in his sophomore season, was old news. Sam Bradford, a sophomore quarterback at the University of Oklahoma, was the new story. Bradford was extraordinary in 2008, throwing for 50 touchdowns against eight interceptions. Like the Gators, the Sooners were 12–1 entering their bowl game. In all those games, the Sooners never scored fewer than 35 points. Nine times they tallied at least 52 points, putting up at least 61 points in each of their last five wins. Bradford and the Sooners were having one of the most prolific seasons in college history. At the Heisman Trophy ceremony in New York, Bradford was named the winner. He became the second sophomore to win the prestigious individual award—one year after Tebow became the first.

Tebow was at the Heisman Award ceremony as a finalist, finishing third in the balloting behind not only Bradford but also University of Texas quarterback Colt McCoy.

Interestingly, Tebow had the most first-place votes with 309; Bradford had 300 and McCoy had 266. But Bradford and McCoy had way more second-place votes than Tebow. In the Heisman Trophy scoring system, 3 points is awarded for a first-place vote, 2 points for second place, and 1 point for third. For whatever reason, Tebow received very few votes from southwest region voters.

Oddly, Tebow had a vote. All former Heisman Trophy winners are eligible, and Tebow had won the award the previous year. And no, he would not say who he voted for in 2008 or any year since!

After the ceremony, Tebow ran into his coach, Urban Meyer, who was angry at the results. All Tebow said to his coach, according to his autobiography, was "Game on." Tebow was already more focused on team goals than individual accomplishments,

The national championship game matched Tebow and the Florida Gators against the new Heisman Trophy winner, Sam Bradford, and the Oklahoma Sooners. Poor Sam. Tebow threw for 231 yards and two touchdowns and ran for a season-high 109 yards on 22 carries. Florida prevailed 24–14. In the fourth quarters of the two championship games against Alabama and Oklahoma, Tebow didn't throw an incomplete pass. He was a combined 11 of 11 passing for 148 yards and two touchdowns.

Tebow had made a promise and emphatically kept his word. Had the Heisman Trophy election been taken after the bowl games—as many argue it should—Tebow most likely would have won his second in a row.

At the end of his college career, Tebow had his second national college football title. Along the way, he gave a memorable speech following that Ole

Numerous Heisman Trophy winners went on to have undistinguished NFL careers, including Ohio State's Archie Griffin, the only two-time Heisman winner. Others who often make the list of Heisman "Busts" are Eric Crouch, Andre Ware, Rashaan Salaam, Ron Dayne, and Ty Detmer.

Miss loss that has become part of his growing legend. "The Promise" has since been inscribed on a plaque and placed outside the front entrance of the Gators' new football facility at Ben Hill Griffin Stadium.

So, which speech was more significant, Knute Rockne's "Win one for the Gipper?" or Tebow's "The Promise?" Here's a case for "The Promise": Notre Dame only had to win one game for George Gipp, admittedly against undefeated Army. Tebow had to win 10 more. Florida won those 10 games by a combined 338 points, an average margin of victory of almost 34 points! To borrow from the title of the Knute Rockne movie, Tim Tebow was everybody's "All-American." Tim Tebow had become one of the most admired athletes on the planet.

Chapter 6

Starting Over

The Broncos' 2010 draft class was not just about Tim Tebow. Check that. To the media, to kids, parents, and fans from Carlsbad to Fort Lauderdale, it was always about Tebow. But Tebow was not alone when the Broncos' rookie class of 2010 gathered for the first time in late June at the annual NFL rookie symposium. First-year players from all 32 teams traveled to a posh resort in Carlsbad, California for meeting after meeting about NFL procedures, policies, and rules.

One night during some free time, the Broncos' rookies gathered on the resort's golf course. But no one brought golf clubs. They were there for a uniquely designed workout. For starters, the rookies ran the golf course, all 18 holes. They would do push-ups and abdominal crunches at the first tee box, and then run to the first green. They would drop and do push-ups and sit-ups. Run again from the first green to the second tee box, then more push-ups and sit-ups.

""We ran all 18 holes. Sit-ups and abs at every hole." said receiver Demaryius Thomas, the first player drafted by the Broncos that year. "It was hot. It about killed me."

This is what a bunch of rookies, on their first night out together, call fun? One guess about who designed the workout.

"Tebow," Thomas said.

Tebow once had a daily workout regimen of 400 push-ups and 400 sit-ups. Not when he was an adult, but at age 11, as a sixth grader! He would rather have been lifting weights with his older brothers Robby and Peter, but Tim's father thought 11 was too young for weights. Tebow and his father copied the 400–400 routine from Herschel Walker, a Heisman Trophy winner for the University of Georgia in 1982 and 1,500-yard rusher for the Dallas Cowboys in 1988.

"My dad told me about Herschel so my mom brought me to the library," Tebow said in January 2012. "That was one of the coolest things about homeschooling is I could really study a lot of things. So for extra reading my mom would let me do whatever I was interested in, pretty much. So I read about Herschel and how he trained. The only thing I was mad about was I didn't have a hill to run up."

Yes, but 400 push-ups and not 50? And 400 sit-ups, not 100? "It was a mark that was hard to get to, but manageable," Tebow said.

The first time Tebow ran onto the field for an NFL game, he was booed. Then again, the Broncos' first pre-season game of the 2010 season was played in Cincinnati, the heart of Ohio State territory. During Tebow's freshman year at Florida, his Gators crushed the Ohio State Buckeyes, 41–14 in the Bowl Championship Series (BCS) national championship game.

"Yeah, I heard it," Tebow said after the game, laughing. "It got me more excited to go out there and play."

Tebow played well, completing 8 of 13 passes in a 33–24 loss. But that's not what Tebow or Bronco followers will remember about his first professional test. Indelible in their minds was the last play of the game when Tebow hurled himself into the end zone for a touchdown.

The play had everything, except an impact on the outcome of the game. Score or no score, the Broncos were not going to win. And the Bronco team was not going all out to win a meaningless pre-season game.

But nothing about competition is meaningless to Tebow. If they're going to keep score, then Tebow is going to compete. Until the very last second, through the very last play.

With 3 seconds left in the game, the Broncos had the ball at the Cincinnati Bengals' 7-yard line. Tebow fielded the shotgun snap and took off toward the right side of the field. He had a choice: fly headfirst across the goal line, increasing the chances of a touchdown even with an increased risk of injury. Or, Tebow could have protected himself against collision while still trying to score, even if a duck, or cut, or finesse maneuver would have diminished the odds of a touchdown. Either way, the Broncos still would have lost the meaningless pre-season game.

Choice? Anyone who knew Tebow understood there was no choice. Go for the score!

"You've got to choose between a smart decision and toughness," Broncos' cornerback André Goodman said at the time. "But when it's in you, it's in you. It's hard to run it off. I would imagine it's going to be tougher for him to learn that than most quarterbacks. I was watching him pace the sidelines for the first half. You should have seen the look he had. He couldn't wait to get in the game."

Want to feel small? Shake hands with Tebow. At 10 inches, Tebow's hands were the largest among quarterbacks in his 2010 rookie draft class. Among the NFL quarterbacks who took snaps last season, only Brett Favre (10⅜-inches) and Drew Brees (10¼-inches) were larger, as measured from thumb to pinky finger.

"I guess it means I can have a pretty good grip on the football," Tebow said. "I've never been coached on something like that. It's just something where coaches have noticed I have a pretty strong grip."

Tebow smashed his way through, taking a running helmet blast to the left ribs from Cincinnati Bengals linebacker Abdul Hodge. Tebow then ricocheted into safety Kyries Hebert, who was moving in for a tackle from the quarterback's right side.

Tebow held on. Touchdown. But he was also left with severely bruised ribs from Hodge's slam.

Two days after the Bengals game, Tebow participated in two practices on a training camp Tuesday. But he skipped the post-workout conditioning sprints. This was significant because Tebow had never lost a conditioning sprint among offensive players during training camp. He started practice the next day, but within 15 minutes retreated into the locker room clutching his left rib-cage area. As it turned out, it was not so much the rib injury that caused concern, but whether Tebow's physical brand of play would lead to more injuries.

"He has a warrior's mentality," said Broncos safety Brian Dawkins. "Which is good. But at the same time, being able to decipher when and when not to—hopefully he won't have to learn the hard way."

As the Broncos defeats mounted week after week in 2010, Coach Josh McDaniels made tentative plans to play the rookie Tebow in the final two games of the season. Both were at home where the crowd would be strongly behind him. The first game was against the lowly Houston Texans with the NFL's 30th-ranked defense. The second was against the AFC West rival San Diego Chargers.

But McDaniels would not be around to implement his plan. There were several reasons why McDaniels was called into owner Pat Bowlen's office on Monday, Dec. 6, 2010 and fired. The biggest was the sorry record. McDaniels' Broncos had lost 17 of their last 22 games. This skid included a 3–9 mark in 2010.

The Broncos were a proud franchise. They had only five losing seasons in the previous 34 years between 1976 and 2009. The team had played in six Super Bowls during that span, winning two. After a 10–6 loss at Kansas City on Sunday, December 5, Bowlen spent all day Monday returning from his second home in Hawaii. Bowlen knew when he arrived at team headquarters, he would have to admit his mistake by releasing the young head coach he had hired just 23 months before.

McDaniels, the coach who most believed in Tebow as an NFL quarterback, was gone. Running backs coach Eric Studesville was named interim coach.

In Studesville's first game, the Broncos were hammered 43–13 by the Arizona Cardinals in Glendale, Arizona. Broncos quarterback Kyle Orton had his worst game of the season with three interceptions and a lost fumble. Late in the game, Orton suffered an injury.

Orton injury or not, Studesville announced the day after the beat-down in the Arizona desert that Tebow would play in Game 14 at Oakland and finish the season.

That's right. Tim Tebow, the All-American boy, a guy who's idea of cussing is "Aw Shucks," would make his NFL starting debut in a place so menacing, it is infamously referred to as the Black Hole.

In the 90-year history of the NFL, only two quarterbacks —Michael Vick in 2002 and Kordell Stewart in 2000—had rushed for a 40-yard touchdown and thrown for a 30-yard score in the same game. Tebow pulled off this feat in the first quarter of his very first start! It all began when the Broncos' offense faced a hopeless third-and-24 situation from the Raiders' 40-yard line. At that point, the Broncos would discover no situation is hopeless with Tebow.

He took off on a safe quarterback draw.

"Well, um, to be honest," Tebow said, trying to stifle a chuckle at the truth he was about to deliver, "that was a mistake on my part."

Tebow thought it was a "Q" or quarterback draw. That

wasn't the call. Tailback Correll Buckhalter was supposed to run the draw. Instead, after Buckhalter realized he wasn't getting the hand off, he led a synchronized group of superb blocking. Tebow churned and cut through a huge hole, broke a tackle, then another. He got more blocks downfield, then determinedly carried a Raider defender into the end zone.

Touchdown Tebow.

"I think his confidence started coming after that run," said Nnamdi Asomugha, the Raiders' star cornerback. Raiders receiver Louis Murphy played with him at Florida and said, "once Tebow gets a little charge; he's going to be a little more courageous with his play."

On the Broncos' next possession, Tebow, from the Raiders' 33, threw a deep, arching pass into the end zone. The ball went right through the hands of Raiders' cornerback Stanford Routt and fell into the stomach of Broncos receiver Brandon Lloyd, who was on his rear. The acrobatic Lloyd not only caught the ball, replay revealed he kept his derriere in-bounds.

Touchdown Tebow.

The Broncos lost to the Raiders, 39–23. But for Tebow and the team, it was progress. Two months earlier, when Oakland visited Denver, the Raiders had embarrassed the Broncos, 59–14.

Tebow's passing stats in his first NFL start were not great, but acceptable. He completed 8 of 16 passes for 138 yards and a touchdown. He also rushed for 78 yards and a touchdown.

The Broncos could have used Tebow at linebacker, too. In two games against the Raiders in the 2010 season, The Denver defense allowed 98 points and 1,010 yards, an average of 49 points and 505 yards a game. Ouch.

"I like the guy," said Raiders standout defensive tackle Tommy Kelly. "He gets a couple more starts under his belt, he's definitely going to keep D-coordinators up at night. He's got a very bright future."

The first win of Tebow's NFL career in 2010 was like so many he would earn during his magical season of 2011. The day after Christmas, the Broncos trailed the Houston Texans, 17–0 at halftime. Tebow had not played well until that point. The game became "Tebow Time" in the second half. He wound up throwing for 308 yards, including beautiful strikes of 50 yards to Jabar Gaffney and 41 yards to Lloyd. With 3:02 remaining in the game, Tebow reversed field and scored on a 6-yard touchdown scramble to give the Broncos their first lead and the win.

"He is exactly what you thought coming out of college," Houston coach Gary Kubiak said afterwards. "He is a winner. He will find a way to make a play. He will find a way to move the chains. He found a way to win a game today and that is what this league is about."

In his first two NFL starts, Tebow at the very least showed why he had so captivated a football nation the past five years—four years at Florida, and his first year with the Broncos.

"It's the passion," Lloyd said after the game. ""And it's funny how it translates to people who don't play. It's strange because to us players, it's expected to play with a lot of passion. But a lot of us don't play with it. And a lot of us know the difference between guys who really are passionate, and guys who are trying to act that way but are chilling out.

"With Tim, when he calls the play I know he's going to do everything humanly possible to make that play happen. It's crazy having that kind of confidence in a rookie quarterback."

Early in the game, Texas players, like many of Tebow's opponents, hurled a few barbs at the quarterback.

Does Tebow ever retaliate with words of his own?

"No, I am not much of a trash talker," Tebow said during his postgame press conference. "I might throw in a 'God Bless.'"

He caused the otherwise grumpy group of reporters to bust out laughing with that remark.

Although Tebow's hands are huge, conversely, his arm length of 30 ¾ inches is a bit short by NFL quarterback standards. At the 2010 NFL scouting combine, where upcoming rookies are tested and measured before the league's coaches, executives, and scouts, quarterbacks Sam Bradford and Jimmy Clausen each had 32-inch arms. 6-foot, 7-inch Joe Flacco, a rookie in 2008, has a right arm that extends to 32 inches.

Tebow's arm could have measured longer if he didn't throw left-handed.

"From what I remember, my left arm is shorter than my right," Tebow said. "It was something weird like that."

When the Broncos lost their final game in 2010, 33–28 to the San Diego Chargers, Tebow's critics flashed a devilish grin and a "told-you-so" attitude.

Tebow passed poorly for most of that last game. Although, in what would become a pattern throughout his two-year stay in Denver, Tebow became a much better passer late in the game. In the game's final drive, he completed five passes and scored on a 6-yard touchdown run with 26 seconds remaining.

The Broncos then recovered the onside kick and Tebow had time to throw two "Hail Mary" passes to the end zone. They both fell incomplete and the Broncos lost. But some how, some way, Tebow had given his team a chance to win a game that for the most part seemed hopeless.

With Tebow at the helm, there is always hope. He wound up completing just 16 of 36 passes with two interceptions. But Tebow also threw two touchdowns and nearly pulled off a comeback from a 26–7 deficit. True to his reputation and college career, Tebow ran for 94 yards at a position, quarterback, not known for rushing the ball.

"Hey, he's a competitor," Philip Rivers, the Chargers' star quarterback, said afterwards. "He thought he was going to win that game today."

At the very least, Tebow showed enough talent in his three-game audition for the Broncos' new hierarchy to go forward with him as their quarterback.

"I don't know why they wouldn't," said Lloyd, who wound up earning his first Pro Bowl appearance as the Broncos' top receiver. "It was great for him to get these three games in because now he can go into the off-season visualizing the speed of the game. You know he's going to work in the off-season to get better. What he already has is he brings so much passion and desire and will to every single play. I'm impressed."

On the Wednesday after the Broncos' disappointing 2010 season ended with a 4–12 record, the team announced the hiring of former quarterback great John Elway as their new vice president of football operations. Eight days later, Elway named John Fox as the team's new head coach.

The Broncos were about to keep two "watches." For the 2011 season, they would thrive during Tebow Time. Little did Tebow know, though, that his time with the Denver Broncos was on the clock and that time was about to expire.

Chapter 7

Tebowmania

Tim Tebow is famous, no doubt. But a continuing topic of conversation in school hallways and office lunchrooms is, "Why is he so famous?"

Is it that he is both a tough quarterback and a clean-cut All-American guy? Is it because he's so wholesome and charitable that even the most protective of parents would want him to marry their daughter?

Is it his committed, unwavering Christian faith? Is it that he is heavily criticized as a quarterback, yet wins, anyway? Is it the passionate, gladiator style of play he brings to a quarterback position that is otherwise reserved for what is perceived to be pampered passers?

Is it, like many other phenomena, not one thing, but a combination of several factors? A more reliable answer may be to find out what event or events triggered "Tebowmania" in the first place.

Before Tebow's senior year in Jacksonville, ESPN cameras followed his movements for a documentary entitled: *The Chosen One*. Not the easiest banner for an 18-year-old to carry around the campus of Nease High. Tebow was uncomfortable with the showy title, but the publicity from the film did help teammates receive college scholarships.

That is an example of how Tebow handles his enormous fame to the advantage of others. He doesn't seek it out. He doesn't even particularly like it. But he understands there is a greater good. He wants to influence kids by serving as a role model. And so, he will not shy away from publicity that would promote his causes.

When ESPN approached him about filming the documentary, Tebow hesitated. His initial instinct may have been to pass on the opportunity. But he realized that what may have looked like a self-serving promotion to some was actually a benefit for so many others.

Tebow, with his Nease teammates, opened the season in a nationally televised game at Alabama powerhouse Hoover High. Nease lost, 50–29, but the experience was invaluable. Later in his senior season, the ESPN documentary that chronicled Tebow's college recruitment was broadcast to the nation.

That Nease went on to win the Florida state 4A title was the first evidence that Tebow did not buckle under pressure. People don't often think of it this way, but there is pressure in living up to all the accolades, maybe even more so than coping with the criticism and second-guessing.

Imagine the burden on a teenager trying to live up to the expectations of *The Chosen One*. Before he threw his first jump pass in college, Tebow's name was familiar in the households of football fans throughout the country.

Tebow arrived at the University of Florida in January 2006 with the makings of a cult hero. He played sporadically as a freshman that fall—in short-yardage packages or as a change-of-pace quarterback relieving the starter, Chris Leak. Immediately, he became a fan favorite and soon was the most famous Gator on a team that included a dozen future NFL players.

Tebow emerged as a national star in 2007, his first year as a starting quarterback for Florida. He became the first sophomore to win the Heisman Trophy as the best player in college football. On the ESPN broadcast the night of the Heisman ceremony, the Tebow family decided to reveal the story of his difficult birth.

Five players from the 2006 Gators' national championship team eventually became first-round, NFL draft picks: Defensive end Jarvis Moss, defensive back Reggie Nelson, receiver/returner Percy Harvin, defensive end Derrick Harvey, and backup quarterback Tim Tebow. Backup linebacker Brandon Spikes was a second-round pick. Defensive tackle Ray McDonald and receiver Andre Caldwell were selected in the third round.

This story of survival against all odds piqued the interest of not only football fans, but also moms and girlfriends, and dads and brothers who otherwise didn't follow football. This group may not have cared who won the game on Saturday, but were interested in learning how Tebow played personally.

Tebow's fame only grew in 2008 as he led Florida to its second Southeastern Conference title and second national championship in three years. Tebow opted to return to Gainesville as a senior in 2009, and he ended his career as perhaps the best college football player ever.

During his college career, Tebow gained a rabid and intensely loyal fan base. He was beloved by old-school football fans for the way he played the game—tough, and with passion—and by the casual fan, and even non-fan, for his good-guy persona.

This fan base followed him to the NFL and the Denver Broncos.

In just three seasons as the starting quarterback at Florida, Tim Tebow passed for 8,927 yards and 83 touchdowns. He also rushed for 2,478 yards and 49 touchdowns. That's an average of 2,976 passing yards, 826 rushing yards — 3,802 yards in all—and 44 touchdowns a year.

While in college, Tebow decided to promote his fame for the benefit of others. Realizing he was given a platform that could help him reach kids everywhere, Tebow took the unusual step of forming his own charitable foundation. NCAA rules prohibit this action because charities raise money. This may lead to charity groups "paying" college student athletes for services rendered, which is banned by the NCAA.

Despite the rules, Tebow was determined to set up his charity. He enlisted several other students to form "First and 15" under the umbrella of the university's student government. The NCAA approved this arrangement.

First and 15 raised money for Uncle Dick's Orphanage—named for a beloved family friend from Tebow's youth—in the Philippines and for a pediatric cancer hospital in Gainesville, the location of the University of Florida. The foundation also arranged Disney World trips for disadvantaged children.

After joining the Denver Broncos, he formed the Tim Tebow Foundation. According to the foundation website, its mission is to bring "faith, hope, and love to those needing a brighter day in their darkest hour of need." This includes the W15H Program, which tries to fulfill the dreams of children with life-threatening illnesses. Another program is Timmy's Playrooms, which are built in children's hospitals all over the world. Uncle Dick's Orphanage in the Philippines still benefits from Tebow's charitable work.

"My passion is growing for my foundation," Tebow said during a private interview in January 2012. "I always wanted to be involved in helping people. But to see where our foundation has gone—I know for the rest of my life I'm going to be involved with that."

Tebow believes he should always use his platform as a football player to honor and do the work of God. Not everyone is comfortable with his viewpoint. But Tebow is unwavering in his Christian faith.

After his electrifying 2011 season with the Broncos ended with a playoff loss at New England, CBS Sports approached Tebow about joining its studio show as a NFL commentator. Tebow had zero interest. Beyond publicity, he didn't see any benefit.

"You could make a pitch to me about why it would be good by saying we could talk about your foundation or you could bring one of your kids," Tebow said. "If they really knew me, they would try to go that way. But then they're like, it would be great pub for me. And I'm like, why is that going to intrigue me?"

When Tebow was selected in the first round of the 2010 NFL draft, No. 25 overall, the commercial side of Tebowmania exploded. Although Tebow was only a Bronco for eight days in April, his No. 15 Broncos jersey was the No. 1 seller for the month on the NFL website.

Two months into the 2010 NFL season through Halloween, Tebow had yet to throw a pass in a regular season game. Yet, his jersey was still No. 1 in sales. At that time, future Hall of Fame quarterback Brett Favre had thrown 10,000 more passes and 500 more touchdowns than Tebow. But when it came to jersey sales, even the popular and respected Favre was no Tebow.

After his rookie season, Tebow released his autobiography, "Through My Eyes." It immediately soared up the national bestseller lists.

Tebowmania soared even higher from an incident that neither involved Tebow personally nor related to an event on the gridiron. Jared Kleinstein, a recent arrival from Denver, left a trendy upscale New York City restaurant and knelt in prayer on East 15th Street. Kleinstein's random act became known as "Tebowing."

When Kleinstein placed a photo of his pose on Facebook, his online friends passed it on to others. And on. And on. Soon, the photo went viral.

"Tebowing" was sweeping a nation.

The Tebow "praying" fad was ignited by one of the most dramatic comebacks in NFL history. And it was all part of Tebow's first start of the 2011 season.

> **"Tebowing" Defined:** To get down on one knee and start praying even if everyone else around you is doing something completely different.

The Broncos record was a weak 1–4 when their coach John Fox decided Tebow's strong showing in the second half against the San Diego Chargers in Game 5 should be rewarded. Following a bye week during which Tebow would get two weeks of practice, he would start Oct. 23 at Miami against the winless Dolphins.

As further evidence of Tebow's popularity, the Dolphins used his appearance to honor the University of Florida's 2008 national championship team. Tebow was the top star of that team. That the Dolphins would essentially honor a visiting player spoke to both Tebow's popularity in Florida —and Miami's struggle to sell tickets to patrons in the state of Florida.

The Dolphin game had been a nightmare for Tebow. As the game entered its final minutes, he had completed just 4 of 14 passes for 40 yards. He was also sacked five times for losses of 27 yards. Those statistics meant the Broncos' passing game through the first 3 ½ quarters was a paltry 13 yards. The Broncos were down 15–0 with 5 minutes and 23 seconds remaining and showing no signs of offensive life.

And then the game became Tebow Time.

In the final 2 minutes and 44 seconds of the fourth quarter, Tebow threw two touchdown passes. He also ran in the crucial 2-point conversion with 17 seconds left to tie the game, 15–15.

In overtime, Broncos placekicker Matt Prater nailed a 52-yard field goal and as his teammates mobbed him in a wild celebration on the field, Tebow first kneeled on the sidelines to give thanks. The television cameras, which beamed the game to a national audience, caught Tebow praying among the bedlam.

Football fans everywhere were excited, too. To quote Tebow fan Jared Kleinstein:

"It's contagious. Love him or hate him, but Tebow fever is contagious."

The "Tebowing" craze spread across America during the week of Halloween 2011. Sports and entertainment celebrities from "Glee" actress Diana Agron to NBA star Dwight Howard to Olympic skier Lindsey Vonn were pictured kneeling, right elbow bent, right fist leaning against the forehead.

Tebow was unsure about how to react to the fad at first. He realized some started "Tebowing" as a mocking gesture. He was also aware as part of his Christian faith that everyone should honor God and Jesus Christ, and not false idols.

But one incident put Tebowing in a better light for him. Tebow learned about a young cancer patient, Joey Norris, who was shown Tebowing during chemotherapy. Joey tweeted: "Tebowing while chemo-ing." This was another example of how Tebow's popularity was not just for him to enjoy, but for the good of others. Tebow, through his

---

Months after "Tebowmania" swept the country, his name still made news. On ESPN's Sportscenter for a period of 10 days in January 2012, Tebow's name was mentioned 154 times, according to Deadspin.com. That was about three times more than the 54 references to the next-most-cited athlete, Green Bay Packers quarterback Aaron Rodgers. Tebow's name was uttered more often than the words: did, been, then, and your.

W15H Program, invited Joey to be his guest for the Broncos' final game of the 2011 regular season.

"It's not my job to see peoples' reasons behind it, but I know (of a kid) with cancer that tweeted me, 'Tebowing while I'm chemoing',—how cool is that?" Tebow said. "That's worth it right now. If that gives him any encouragement or puts a smile on his face, or gives him encouragement to pray, that's completely awesome."

Tebow became so well-known that NBC's long-time hit comedy show, *Saturday Night Live*, featured a Tebow character in a skit that spoofed his Christian beliefs. Tebow was more concerned about how his religion, rather than he, was treated. As usual, he took the high road

"I did see it," he said a month after the SNL skit aired. "I didn't want to finish watching it. I feel like I can laugh at myself pretty well but ... Patrick (Smyth, the Broncos' media relations director) and I have talked about it a few times that the greatest form of flattery is impersonation. I guess you have to take it with a grain of salt. It's all right. At least they're talking about it, talking about Jesus."

Tebow: He has taken a sledgehammer to the notion that born-again Christian athletes are too soft. That they have too much peace and joy in their heart to be rough, tough competitors against their fellow man.

"It's so the opposite," Tebow said in that January 2012 interview. "As a Christian it's not about being soft. Jesus Christ was the toughest guy ever. The beating he had to take. And then, not only that but to take on the sin of the

Saturday Night Live is a late-night comedy and variety show that was first broadcast on NBC in October 1975. Guest hosts have included current NFL quarterbacks Peyton Manning and Eli Manning. The skit that mocked Tebow's wholesomeness and Christian fervor aired in December 2011. Tebow, who did not appear on the show, was played by SNL regular Tiran Killam.

world for you, that's a lot worse. But as a Christian, that sometimes bothers me that Christians are always soft.

"As a Christian you should be kind and turn the other cheek, but at the same time you need to be the toughest one, you need to be the one setting an example, you need to show character, you need to be the one working hard. Because so many times in the Bible it talks about whatever we do, do with all your might, do unto the Lord."

Chapter 8

The Chance to Start

The Denver Broncos finished the 2010 season with 4 wins and 12 losses, tied for the second-worst record in the NFL. Included in that mark was a 1–2 record in the three, season-ending starts by rookie quarterback Tim Tebow.

The team's decision makers for most of that year—coach Josh McDaniels and general manager Brian Xanders—agreed that Tebow showed enough promise in his three-game audition to project him as the starting quarterback in 2011.

But there was a new set of eyes with a new mindset now in charge of the Broncos' football operations. John Elway, the team's Hall of Fame quarterback, had been hired to head the team's front office three days after the end of the 2010 season. A week later, on Jan. 13, 2011, Elway, Xanders,

John Fox was the complete opposite of his predecessor, Josh McDaniels, in age, coaching experience, and personality. When McDaniel was hired, he was only 32 years old, with no head coaching experience. On the other hand, Fox was almost 56 years old and had been head coach the previous nine seasons with the Carolina Panthers. Fox was also friendly and jovial, and well-liked by the NFL media, players, and coaching fraternity. McDaniels was friendly, but more reserved with a volatile streak.

team president Joe Ellis, and Bowlen named John Fox the Broncos' new head coach.

From Day 1, Elway and Fox had to settle the controversy at starting quarterback between the veteran Kyle Orton and young Tebow. Orton was a decent but hardly outstanding NFL quarterback. Elway and Fox were uncertain about Tebow, good or bad. Tebow, remember, is the type of unorthodox quarterback who can confound the cleverest of football minds.

There was no question about where General Manager Brian Xanders stood on the issue. He liked what he saw from Tebow in 2010. He believed Tebow had shown enough ability to compete for the starting role in 2011.

Xanders believed Tebow raised the level of play of his teammates. Certainly, Tebow would have growing pains as a passer. But as Tebow developed and improved, Xanders was confident the young lefty could figure out how to win a few games, at the very least.

Xanders thought for the long-term good of the team it was important to find out sooner rather than later whether Tebow was a starting quarterback in the NFL. This meant trading Orton.

If Fox was uneasy about Tebow's progress in training camp and the pre-season, the team could always turn to a third quarterback on the roster, Brady Quinn. A first-round draft pick by Cleveland in 2007 who started 12 games in 2008–09, Quinn would have become a capable stopgap in the position until Tebow was ready to start.

On the first full day Elway was on the job, Orton asked for a trade. Orton told his new boss that he did not want to go through a second season dealing with what came to be known as "The Tebow Circus." This referred to the massive media attention and fan adulation Tebow received.

Orton sensed the Broncos were leaning toward Tebow. Coming off three straight seasons as an NFL starting quarterback, Orton believed he should not have to sit on the bench in favor of the unproven Tebow.

So, a plan was devised. The Broncos would trade Orton. Tebow would become the Broncos' starting quarterback but would receive competition in training camp and the pre-season from Quinn.

There was just one problem: A labor disagreement between the owners and players union put the NFL off-season on "lock down." This meant teams could not sign free agent players or make trades. The lockdown was officially called a "lock out" because the players were barred from entering any of the team's facilities.

The Broncos could not trade Orton until the labor dispute was resolved. The owners and players did finally settle their issues and the NFL season was back on—but just two days before the start of training camp.

Orton was put on the trading block Tuesday, July 26. Training camp would begin two days later. Although several teams were in the quarterback market, only the Miami Dolphins viewed Orton as their No. 1 choice.

The Dolphins were eager to acquire Orton but only if the quarterback would agree to a new contract. The two sides thought a deal was in place but the Dolphins suddenly changed their mind and pulled out.

When training camp opened two days later on July 28, Orton was still a Bronco. Worse for Tebow, Fox had tabbed Orton as the No. 1 quarterback, at least for the start of training camp.

In a matter of hours, Tebow went from expected opening-day starter of 2011 to backup.

"My reaction? Well, time to go compete," Tebow said at season's end. "I wasn't down at all. You don't ever want to be handed anything. And it wouldn't have been that way because Brady would have been competing. You want to earn it. You want to prove yourself in a game and earn that way. Not, 'Hey, we're going to trade him and try to make it easier.' No, I was fine with it."

Unfortunately for Tebow, his situation would get worse

before it got better. Orton outperformed Tebow in practice. Then, through the first two pre-season games, the other back-up quarterback, Brady Quinn, played well.

Entering the final pre-season game at Arizona, Tebow, for the first time in his life, was a No. 3 quarterback. He had endured the experience of a coach wanting him to play running back or linebacker. He survived the times when football's brightest minds said he couldn't make it as a quarterback. He had been a backup quarterback both as a freshman at Florida and rookie in the NFL.

But never had Tebow been No. 3 on the team's quarterback depth chart. Tebow simply wasn't throwing the ball well enough in training camp practices. Tebow, remember, has the reputation of a "gamer," not necessarily a practice player. He plays his best at the most crucial junctures of the game.

"I guess from the outside looking at it, as a competitor, it can be a little frustrating," he said at season's end. "But I believe that when we actually play a real football game, I can play the game of football. When we're out there and don't play with pads and it's 7 on 7, it's a lot different. I just couldn't wait for the chance to go play in a game. In the pre-season I thought I played pretty well. In games."

In the final pre-season game against the Arizona Cardinals, Quinn played poorly in the first half. Tebow had his opportunity. With Arizona ahead 26-0 and just 4:33 remaining in the game and the Broncos backed up to their 6-yard line, fans got their first demonstration of "Tebow Time" in 2011.

Although an effective scrambler by nature, Tebow avoided the run during this drive. Instead, he came through with his best performance from the passing pocket since he was drafted by the Broncos.

From the pocket and near his own end zone, Tebow calmly, yet daringly, threw a deep touch pass to D'Andre Goodwin for a 26-yard gain. Later, Tebow converted a third-and-10 with a completion to Eron Riley. Then Tebow, who always has been a better-than-average deep-ball thrower, tossed a perfect strike to Riley for a 43-yard touchdown.

The way the drive played out, it was almost as if Broncos offensive coordinator Mike McCoy told Tebow: Don't run. We want to see you stay in the pocket and pass.

Asked if McCoy told him not to run during that final pre-season drive, Tebow said: "No, it just worked out that way. I remember thinking after the first play of that drive, this isn't the time to try and get first downs or score. It's time to show I could go through my progressions. So after that I was thinking, "They know I can make a play, I need to try and show another part of the quarterback arsenal.""

Although just a pre-season game, it was a huge series for Tebow. Had he not performed well on that 94-yard scoring drive, he would have started the season as the No. 3 quarterback—behind Orton and Quinn. And had Quinn been No. 2, he would have been the first one in after Orton struggled through the first five games of the regular season. Not Tebow.

Had Tebow failed late in the Arizona game, he may never have had a chance to succeed, let alone play, during the magical 2011 season.

"Absolutely a fair statement," Tebow said. "You never know what's going to happen. NFL—Not For Long."

The first regular-season game of the John Elway–John Fox era ended in disappointment as the Broncos lost at home on Monday night to their rival Oakland Raiders, 23–20.

Orton did not play well in the first half as the Broncos fell behind 16–3. Later, when the team had a chance to rally for victory, Orton rolled right and had tight end Daniel Fells wide open down field on the left side. But on a drizzly night, the ball slipped out of Orton's hand and the Raiders recovered the fumble.

Many Bronco players were injured in the Raider game and in their second game against the Cincinnati Bengals. When receiver Eddie Royal and tight end Julius Thomas went down with injuries early in the Bengal game, the Broncos were left with just two healthy receivers.

So, Fox inserted Tebow into the lineup to play receiver, almost unprecedented for a quarterback. He was only in for three plays at receiver, and Orton did not throw a pass Tebow's way

"Oh, man, I wanted one so bad," Tebow said later. "The first play I was in, Kyle audibled to a draw, I believe, and I would have had an in-route. I would have had a chance to get the ball, too."

The following week, against a physical Tennessee Titan team in Nashville, the Broncos were in control most of the game, but lost 17-14. An Orton pass was intercepted on the final drive.

The next week at Green Bay, Orton threw an early interception that was returned for a touchdown and the Broncos were trounced by the Packers, 49-23, at Lambeau Field.

That loss left the Broncos with 1 win and 3 losses. When Orton played poorly again the next week against the San Diego Chargers—completing just 6 of 13 passes for 34 yards and an interception in the first half—Tebow replaced him at quarterback to start the third quarter.

Down 26-10 midway through the fourth quarter, Tebow brought the Broncos back to life. He scored on a 12-yard touchdown run with 6:35 remaining, then hit running back Knowshon Moreno for a 28-yard catch-and-run score with 3:19 left.

Suddenly, the Broncos were within 2 points at 26-24. The sellout crowd in Denver was frenzied. On the 2-point conversion, Tebow threw a perfect fade pass to the end

During the bye week, the Broncos' best receiver was traded. Brandon Lloyd sensed the team would go to a run-oriented offensive attack which meant he would likely catch fewer passes. The Broncos met Lloyd's trade request by dealing him to the St. Louis Rams in return for a conditional sixth-round draft pick. The condition? If Lloyd caught 30 passes the rest of the season with the Rams, the Broncos would instead get a fifth-round pick. Lloyd wound up with 51 catches for the Rams and the Broncos wound up taking Tennessee defensive end Malik Jackson with their fifth-round selection in the 2012 draft.

zone, but receiver Brandon Lloyd couldn't hang on. The Chargers won, 29–24.

After a bye week, Tebow would get his first start of the season two weeks later against division rival, the Miami Dolphins.

After leading the Broncos past the Dolphins for a dramatic, 18–15 win in overtime in his first start, Tebow struggled the next week against the much improved Detroit Lions. The Broncos were behind 24–3 at halftime. The second half didn't go much better. Early in the third quarter, Lions defensive end Cliff Avril stripped the ball

In the decade between the start of the 2001 season and the end of the 2010 season, the Lions were an NFL laughingstock. They were 2–14 in 2001, followed by records of 3–13, 5–11, 6–10, 5–11, 3–13, and 7–9 (losing seven of their last eight). In 2008 they became the first team in NFL history to go 0–16.

The Lions then selected quarterback Matthew Stafford as the No. 1 overall pick in the 2009 draft. After going 2–14, the Lions opened 2–10 in 2010 before winning their final four games. Stafford and star receiver Calvin Johnson led Detroit to a 10–6 record and playoff appearance in 2011, their best season in 16 years.

away from Tebow from behind, picked up the fumble, and ran it in for a touchdown. Tebow later threw an interception that Lions defensive back Chris Houston returned 100 yards for a touchdown, and the Broncos were down 45–3.

As is his nature, Tebow didn't give up. About anyone can play hard when he's ahead or the score is close. But how many players can honestly say they give it their all even when defeat is certain?

Tebow, that's who. Despite the embarrassment of a "pick six"—an interception run back for a touchdown by the defense—Tebow led the Broncos on an 80-yard touchdown drive on their next possession. The drive ended with Tebow throwing a 14-yard touchdown pass to Eric Decker.

His late-game performance wasn't enough to convince Coach Fox to stick with Tebow. Fox revealed after the game that if Tebow played as poorly as he did against the Lions and Dolphins despite the miraculous victory, Tebow might be replaced as starting quarterback.

Fox would give Tebow the first half of the next game to perform well or be replaced. Unfortunately, that game was on the road against the dreaded Oakland Raiders in the infamous "Black Hole." Gulp!

A Black Hole is a deadly area in outer space so dense that its gravitational forces prevent anything that comes close enough from escaping. The Raiders wound up calling a specific section of their Oakland Coliseum home "The Black Hole." It's the section where fans often wear face paint, masks, and intimidating costumes. The fans are among the rowdiest in the country. With such fans spreading throughout the stadium over the years, the Raiders entire stadium—often renamed to represent various sponsors—is now frequently referred to as "The Black Hole."

Whether Fox was serious about pulling Tebow is unknown. What is known is that besides his threat, Fox had his offensive coordinator Mike McCoy install the spread, read-option offense for the Raiders' game. In the read-option, Tebow stood in the shotgun and had the option to either hand the ball off to the tailback or keep it himself. On some plays, he also had the option to pass the ball.

It was a similar offense that Tebow operated at the University of Florida, to enormous success. Would Fox have installed the offense that was so specific to Tebow's unique skill set if he was serious about pulling him? Probably not.

Chapter 9

The Option and Rex

When the Broncos faced the New York Jets in Denver on Nov. 17, 2011, Tim Tebow had already become the most talked about player in the NFL. The Broncos had won two in a row and were 3–1 with Tebow as their starting quarterback.

The Jets had reached the AFC championship game the previous two seasons, losing both times. In 2011, the team was struggling to meet the expectations that came with the prediction of a Jets Super Bowl triumph in 2011. That prediction came from the outspoken Jets head coach Rex Ryan.

The regular season match-up between the Broncos and the Jets was all the more special because it would be the only game played that Thursday night. It would also be

Jets' coach Rex Ryan is the son of former NFL defensive coordinator and head coach Buddy Ryan. The Ryan family—Rex's brother Rob is the Dallas Cowboys' defensive coordinator—is known for speaking their minds. In an NFL world where coaches are often overly cautious when answering questions, Ryan's candor is considered refreshing. In February, 2011, Ryan predicted his Jets would win the Super Bowl. Instead, they finished 8–8 and missed the playoffs. Ryan later regretted his bold prediction because it may have put too much pressure on his team to win.

televised by the NFL Network. Avid Jet fan Ray Romano, star of the long-running TV sitcom "Everybody Loves Raymond," was on the Jets' sideline with his sons before the game.

The biggest reason for the public's interest in the game did not come from anyone on the Jets side. It was Tebow. This would be his first NFL start in a game that was nationally televised. Millions of fans wanted to see for themselves what all the fuss was about.

Just when you thought there were no more twists to the Tim Tebow story, along comes another unexpected turn. When the Broncos dusted off the old-fashioned, run-only option offense and handily beat the Oakland Raiders 38–24—NFL fans across the country were fascinated.

In this era of sophisticated passing attacks, when NFL quarterbacks regularly throw for 300 yards a game, how in the name of "Woody Hayes" can a team win by running the option?

A team that has Tebow at quarterback, that's who.

While running the option formation against the Raiders, the Broncos rushed for 299 yards. Tebow had 117 yards rushing and halfback Willis McGahee finished with 163. Tebow and McGahee became the Broncos' first quarterback–running back combination to each rush for 100 yards in the same game since Norris Weese and Otis Armstrong pulled off the feat in a Dec. 12, 1976 game.

When was the last time Raiders' eight-year veteran quarterback Carson Palmer had seen a read-option offense?

"I think it was college," he said.

Sometimes, innovation is having the guts to do what has already been done. What can be considered "old" to college football may be "new" to the NFL.

Woody Hayes was Ohio State's iconic head coach from 1951 through 1978. His contempt for the passing game is epitomized by his famous quote: "Only three things can happen when you pass the ball and two of them are bad." (The two bad things are an incompletion and an interception. The one good thing is a completion.) In a memorable 1973 matchup against rival Michigan, Ohio State, ranked No. 1 in the country, had zero passing yards in a 10–10 tie.

Hayes unceremoniously lost his job, ironically, after one of those two bad things happened with a forward pass. In the 1978 Gator Bowl, Hayes' quarterback Art Schlichter was intercepted by Clemson's Charlie Bauman. Hayes came off the sideline and punched Bauman in the throat. Ohio State fired Hayes the next day.

ESPN and the NFL Network spent the week breaking down the Tebow-led read option. On several plays, Broncos offensive coordinator Mike McCoy designed plays that gave Tebow the option: From the shotgun, the lefty quarterback could either hand off to McGahee, or keep it himself and run around end.

Tebow not only ran the Raiders silly around end, he threw touchdown passes of 27 yards to Eric Decker and 26 yards to Eddie Royal.

It was another clutch Tebow performance because for the first time in his NFL career, he was challenged with the loss of his starting job. Head coach John Fox had indicated in the days before the game he would replace Tebow if he was playing poorly. That Tebow responded didn't surprise those who knew him well.

"Honestly, I put that pressure on myself more than anybody else," Tebow remarked after the game. "To try and improve and ultimately get a victory no matter how it looks. That was a special one."

When asked if he was ready to name Tebow as his starter the following week at Kansas City, Coach Fox did not hesitate this time: "Yes I can."

In the following week's game against the Chiefs, the Broncos running attack clicked again. The Broncos ran the ball 55 times even though their top two running backs, McGahee and Knowshon Moreno, suffered first-quarter injuries and did not return. No problem. The Broncos called 30 rushing attempts for No. 3 tailback Lance Ball.

Tebow ran the ball, including rushing for a touchdown on the Broncos first possession. He pitched the ball. He handed off the ball. He even faked a few passes before handing off.

Tebow did not complete a pass until more than 12 minutes were played in the third quarter. Tebow had gone more than a full game without a passing yard. In the previous week's win at Oakland, Tebow threw his last pass, a 29-yard completion to Demaryius Thomas, with 6:38 remaining in the third quarter. The Broncos finished that game with 19 consecutive plays without a pass attempt. In the game against the Chiefs, the Broncos ran 14 plays in the first quarter. All were runs.

In all, the Broncos ran 33 consecutive plays without a pass attempt—32 runs and one sack—until Tebow opened the second quarter against the Chiefs by heaving a deep incompletion downfield.

Tebow was 0 for 5 with 3:58 remaining in the third quarter when he flipped a safe, short pass to Matt Willis for a 13-yard gain. Add it up and Tebow went four quarters and nearly 3 minutes of game clock without a completion.

With less than 7 minutes remaining in the game, Tebow was 1 of 7 passing for 13 yards. And the Chiefs had closed to 10–7. And then, as only Tebow can seemingly do in the fourth quarter, the lefty whipped a beautiful 56-yard touchdown pass to Decker, who beat the lulled Chiefs' secondary to sleep. The Broncos had won, 17–10, their third consecutive road triumph with Tebow at quarterback.

For most of the game against the Jets, a prime time audience could not have been overly impressed with the phenomenon that was Tebow. The Jets were ahead 13–10 with about 6 minutes left in the game. The Broncos were pinned on their own 5-yard line, 95 yards from a score.

As usual, there was little indication Tebow was capable of leading the Broncos downfield. He was just 1 of 8 passing in the third quarter, and had run just twice for 11 yards.

It appeared Ryan's Jets had finally solved the Tebow puzzle that had stupefied the NFL. Then, Ryan had a rude introduction to "Tebow Time." In that final 6 minutes, Tebow was unstoppable. He ran six times for 57 yards. He completed 3 of 5 passes for 35 yards. Add it up and Tebow accounted for 92 yards on the Broncos' final 95-yard drive.

When Ryan called for an all-out blitz, Tebow got around safety Eric Smith and raced 20 yards for a touchdown with 58 seconds remaining. The Broncos won 17–13. A sellout crowd of 74,746 was delirious with joy. The national cable audience was incredulous that Tebow had done it again, pulling victory from almost certain defeat.

Five months later, the quarterback who beat Ryan that day had now joined him. Tebow was a New York Jet.

Chapter 10

Critics, Many Silenced

To recognize that Tim Tebow is, perhaps, the most popular athlete in America tells only half the story. The other half is that Tebow is probably also the most criticized player. More accurately, Tebow is regarded by many as football's most polarizing player. This means most fans either really like or really dislike him. There's no in-between.

His popularity is easy to understand. The criticism is often baffling. Tebow never says a bad word about anybody. It's obvious that whether he's playing well or not-so-well that he gives it his all.

Most of all, Tebow is a winner. No matter how poorly a game is going, he never quits and often figures out how to win at the end. Yet, NFL analysts like Jimmy Johnson, Shannon Sharpe, Trent Dilfer, and Joe Theismann, among others, questioned whether Tebow was consistent enough to succeed because of major flaws in his passing motion.

When it came to Tebow, even active players broke the unwritten code that you don't criticize other players, including opponents. Baltimore linebacker Terrell Suggs joined active players Steve Smith, Jermichael Finley, and Joe Flacco in ripping Tebow. But no one was more mean-spirited than Merrill Hoge, former NFL running back and current ESPN analyst. In August 2011, while the Broncos were still in training camp and had yet to play their first pre-season game, Hoge tweeted:

"It's embarrassing to think the Broncos could win with Tebow!"

A few months later, after Tebow had directed the Broncos to their first playoff appearance in six years, it was Hoge who blushed.

After Tebow's remarkable 20-yard touchdown run with 58 seconds left beat the New York Jets, 17–13 on Nov. 17, the lefty who critics said couldn't play quarterback had led the Broncos to three wins in a row. He was 4–1 as a starter for a team that was 1–4 before he took control.

Yet, Tebow magic was only at its halfway point that season. In a road game at San Diego against AFC West rival the Chargers on Nov. 27, Tebow led the Broncos back from a 10–0 deficit. He engineered late scoring drives in the first half (an 18-yard touchdown pass), in the fourth quarter (a short field goal by Matt Prater with 1:34 remaining), and in overtime (a 37-yard field goal by Prater with 29 seconds left).

The following week at Minnesota, Tebow again played poorly early in the game. The Broncos' offense had just one first down while falling behind 15–7 at halftime.

"Tebow Time" kicked in at the start of the second half. Although he only had six more completions for the whole game, the passes went for 178 yards, including two touchdown strikes to Demaryius Thomas. The Broncos won another close one, 35–32 on Matt Prater's short, walk-off field goal.

"I mean, the dude lit us up," Vikings star defensive end Jared Allen said about Tebow. "I would have bet my paycheck that he would not have beat us passing the ball. Hats off to him."

Remarkably, the Broncos were now tied with the Oakland Raiders for the AFC West lead with 7–5 records. The following week against the Chicago Bears, the Broncos were down 10–0 with just 2 minutes, 15 seconds remaining in the game. Tebow threw a touchdown pass to Demaryius Thomas, but the Broncos were still down 10–7 when they got the ball back at their own 20-yard line with just 56 seconds remaining.

It isn't until the final minutes, often the last seconds, of a game that Tebow turns into one of the NFL's most accurate passers. On the first two plays, he completed passes of 9 yards to Eric Decker and 11 yards to Lance Ball. The Broncos were on their own 40-yard line but after Tebow spiked the ball to stop the clock, only 30 seconds remained. He then fired a 19-yard strike to Matt Willis, and the ball was down to the Bears' 41-yard line. That was close enough for Prater's strong leg. He kicked a 59-yard field goal with 3 seconds left to send still another game into overtime. On his first possession in the extra period, Tebow again drove the ball into Bears' territory and Prater again kicked a long-range field goal, this one from 51 yards.

Tebow's Broncos had won six in a row. He was 3–0 in overtime games and 5–0 on the road. Better yet, the Broncos were alone in the AFC West lead with an 8–5 record.

Although the Broncos lost their final three regular season games, they had already done enough to win their division. Their 8–8 record matched that of Oakland and San Diego, but the Broncos won the division in a tiebreaker because of their better conference record.

For the first time since 2005, the Broncos qualified for the playoffs. But few Denver fans seemed very excited. The team was struggling. In his final two games of the season, a 40–14 loss at Buffalo and 7–3 defeat to the Chiefs, Tebow completed just 19 of 51 passes (37.3 percent) with four interceptions.

The loss to the Chiefs was especially galling. The Chiefs were led by former Denver quarterback Kyle Orton, whom the Broncos had earlier released in favor of Tebow. There was a feeling that the magic of the wins earlier in the season was gone, that other teams had learned to control Tebow's unique quarterbacking style.

The Broncos' first-round opponent in the playoffs was the Pittsburgh Steelers, owner of the NFL's best defense. Although the game would be played in Denver, the Steelers were a 9½ point favorite.

Again, Broncos coach John Fox indicated Tebow might be replaced at quarterback at halftime if his poor play of the previous two weeks continued. (Name another quarterback who constantly had to play on such a short leash!)

It was just like Tebow to respond with the best game of his career. In the first half, he threw a 30-yard touchdown pass to Eddie Royal and ran for a touchdown to give the Broncos a 20–6 halftime advantage.

The Steelers rallied in the second half to tie the game, 23–23, forcing Tebow and the Broncos to play their fourth overtime game of the season. On the Broncos first play from scrimmage in the overtime, the Steelers put all 11 defenders within a few yards of the line of scrimmage. Tebow threw a perfect strike across the middle to Thomas, who ran the rest of the way for an 80-yard touchdown.

The Broncos had won 29–23. They were 4–0 in overtime games under Tebow. He had performed miracle after miracle in lifting a team that was arguably the NFL's worst before he became their starting quarterback, to among the league's elite eight teams.

Still, those wins weren't enough to convince Bronco executives that Tebow was their long-term answer at quarterback. For all of his accomplishments, Tebow was the first player the Broncos traded at the end of the 2011 season.

In the stretch between November 1, 2009 and October 23, 2011, the day Tebow started his first game for the Broncos, Denver's 7–24 record was the worst in the NFL. The Broncos lost 8 of their final 10 games in 2009, were 4–12 in 2010, and then 1–4 to start the 2011 season. Tebow then won 7 of his first eight starts of 2011, meaning he generated as many wins in eight games as the Broncos had in their previous 31 games when their quarterback was primarily Kyle Orton.

Chapter 11

Hello, New York!

The New England Patriots marched over the Denver Broncos 45–10, in the second round of the 2011 playoffs at Gillette Stadium in Foxborough, Mass. But the one-sided loss was hardly the fault of Tim Tebow. Early in the third quarter, Patriots quarterback Tom Brady had already tossed a record six touchdown passes against a woeful Broncos' defense. The score at that point was 42–10.

Tebow suffered injuries to his ribs, chest, and shoulder after being sacked in the third quarter. He probably would have been unable to play the following week even if the Broncos had managed to somehow win to reach the AFC championship game.

At the end of the season, Broncos president Joe Ellis approached John Elway, head of football operations, about obtaining superstar Peyton Manning if the all-time great quarterback became a free agent as expected. Elway liked the idea. Elway had been a star quarterback himself, playing in five Super Bowls and winning twice during his playing career from 1983–98. His philosophy was that a team could not reach the Super Bowl without a quarterback winning one or two playoff games through the air. Because of this belief, Elway never warmed to Tebow's quarterback play which featured the run more than the pass.

John Fox approved the idea of acquiring Manning, too. During Fox's 10 seasons as an NFL head coach, he never had a quarterback with Manning's passing skills. Manning had never missed a start in his first 13 NFL seasons with the Indianapolis Colts—a streak of 227 consecutive games including 19 in the playoffs.

But Manning's contract with the Colts called for him to earn a whopping $35.4 million in 2012. This gigantic sum included a $28 million option bonus that was due March 8, 2012. Manning would soon be 36 years old, old for a football player—even a quarterback. His health was suspect after he missed the entire 2011 season with a neck injury.

Under those circumstances, the Colts chose not to pay Manning that $28 million bonus. On March 6, two days before his option bonus was due, the Colts released their beloved and iconic quarterback. This meant any team could sign him at the right price. At least 10 teams showed interest in Manning, neck injury or not. He had led the Colts to the Super Bowl twice, winning once. Even with his missed season, he ranked third all-time in career touchdown passes and passing yards. So, Manning was still in demand, if not by the Colts.

Manning narrowed his choices to four teams—the Broncos, Arizona Cardinals, San Francisco 49ers, and Tennessee Titans. On March 19, Manning informed Elway he wanted to play for the Broncos. The next day, Manning was introduced as the Broncos' new starting quarterback.

Suddenly, Tebow became unwanted by his current team. As expected, on March 21, the Broncos traded him to the New York Jets in exchange for a fourth- and sixth-round draft pick.

Elway, along with the other Bronco executives, believed Tebow would be too much of a distraction to keep as a No. 2 quarterback behind Manning. Tebow had fans everywhere, not just in Denver. Once, when the Broncos were getting routed in a game in Green Bay, Packer fans who wanted to see him play began chanting "Te-bow! Te-bow!"

Whenever Elway or Fox said anything even slightly critical of Tebow's play, his supporters would fight back by unloading harsher criticism on the Bronco bosses. Elway may have been a legendary Broncos quarterback, but as an executive he would occasionally play the role of villain to fans who believed Tebow deserved greater support.

The Broncos wanted to turn over their franchise to Peyton Manning without any distractions. And so Tebow—the person most responsible for bringing excitement back to the Broncos and for turning what had been a terrible team into a playoff contender—became the first player the Broncos pushed out the door.

That Tebow became a Jet was no surprise. The Jacksonville Jaguars were also interested, but Tebow preferred New York over his hometown team primarily because the Jets offered him a greater promise to play. In Jacksonville, Tebow might have been the No. 3 quarterback behind Blaine Gabbert, the No. 10 overall draft pick in 2011, and recently signed free agent Chad Henne, who had started the previous three seasons in Miami.

With the Jets, Tebow would be the No. 2 quarterback behind three-year starter Mark Sanchez. Besides that, Jets Coach Rex Ryan and general manager Mike Tannenbaum promised to use Tebow as a running quarterback in the so-called "wildcat" formation in each game.

The Jets remembered the first time they saw Tebow, in October 2010, when he rushed for a touchdown against them. At the time, the Jets were ranked No. 1 in rushing and the Broncos were ranked 32nd, or last in the NFL, with just 51.8 yards per game. With Tebow adding his wrinkle, the Broncos amassed 145 yards—enough to outgain the Jets, who were held to 129 yards.

The Jets' running game went stagnant in 2011 after losing their "wildcat" player Brad Smith to free agency and Buffalo.

Coach Ryan is known as a defensive specialist. And defensive-minded head coaches want their offense to run the ball. Running the ball chews up the game clock—and keeps the defense rested on the sideline. The best defense is a defense watching from the bench.

But Tebow will not be satisfied merely in a "wildcat" role, as just a running quarterback. He wants to be a quarterback, period, which includes passing to win.

"I think, first and foremost, I'm a football player first and then a quarterback, although that is my dream, that's what I want to be," Tebow said at his introductory Jets' press conference. "That's what I believe I am, is a quarterback. But however I can help the team, however I can make a difference, however they can use me, I'll be open to it and work as hard as I can every time I step on that field. I would give my whole heart to be the best Jet I possibly can be and help this team win football games."

To do that, Tebow would have to improve his 46% completion rate as a passer. It would be a challenge, but no more than other obstacles Tebow has faced during his life.

Take the Tim Tebow Challenge!

1. Tebow was born in (a) Jacksonville, FL (b) the Philippines (c) Denver, CO (d) a football uniform

2. Tebow graduated from what high school? (a) Peace (b) Nease (c) Meese (d) Reese's Pieces

3. True or False: Tebow won only one Super Bowl with the Denver Broncos.

4. Tebow's famous locker room speech to his Florida teammates became known as (a) The Promise (b) The Pledge (c) The Statement (d) The Fib

5. The sports nickname for the University of Florida is (a) Seminoles (b) Gators (c) Horned Frogs (d) Mutant Ninja Turtles

6. The Tebow craze that swept America is called (a) Tebow-wow! (b) Tim Time! (c) Tebowmania! (d) Linsanity!

7. Tebow said his unusual passing delivery is the result of (a) an arm injury (b) baseball pitching (c) weight lifting (d) juggling anvils

8. The Heisman Trophy is awarded each year to (a) the best collegiate football player (b) the most valuable player in the NFL (c) the best quarterback in America (d) some guy named Heisman

9. Tebow was gently mocked on what comedy TV show in December 2011? (a) Jimmy Kimmel Live (b) The Colbert Report (c) Saturday Night Live (d) Two-and-a-Half Tebows

10. Tebow's brothers are named (a) Robby and Peter (b) Kyle and Brady (c) Peyton and Eli (d) Homer and Bart

ANSWERS

1. **b** Tebow was born in a hospital outside of Manila.
2. **b** Ponte Vedra Beach Nease High School, outside of Jacksonville, FL
3. **False** Tebow has not won a Super Bowl...yet.
4. **a** "The Promise" is the topic of Chapter 6.
5. **b** Florida is the home to over 1 million alligators.
6. **c** "Tebowmania" is discussed in Chapter 7.
7. **b** Tebow's delivery is long, like a baseball pitcher.
8. **a** Tebow won the award in 2010.
9. **c** Tebow did not appear on the show himself.
10. **a** Robby and Peter are Tim's older brothers.

For every correct answer, you gain "10 yards." Add the number of correct answers and yards for your result:

90–100 yards TOUCHDOWN!

70–80 yards FIELD GOAL

60–70 yards FIRST DOWN

under 60 yards FUMBLE

About the Author

As the oldest son of Joseph and Mary (Ann), Mike Klis can relate to the burdens of Tim Tebow. A graduate of Oswego (Ill.) High School and Murray (Ky.) State University, Klis got his start as a sports writer in the early 1980s with the *Oswego Ledger-Sentinel*, where he covered high school sports and the town's men's slo-pitch softball league.

He later worked in Colorado as news editor for the *Fountain Valley Advertiser* (1985), sports editor for the *Woodland Park's Ute Pass Courier* (1986), and sports reporter for the *Colorado Springs Gazette Telegraph* (part-time from 1984–87; full-time 1987–1998).

He joined *The Denver Post* as a Colorado Rockies–Major League Baseball writer in January, 1998. He was moved to the Broncos' beat in July 2005.

He has three sisters (Lori, Kathy, Sherri), two brothers (Tom and Bryan), a goddaughter (Annie), three nephews (Patrick, Joey, Timmy), and three nieces (Adrianne, Annie, Josie).

Klis and his wife Becky have four children: Brittney, Kaitlyn, Blake, and Johnny.

This is Klis' second book on Tebow. The first, *Will To Win*, is available on *www.denverpost.com*.